A joyful and effective guide to increasing vitality, comfort and enjoyment of life in later years. Mary Dale Scheller shows us that it's never too late to cultivate better health and wholeness.

M A R T I N   L .   R O S S M A N ,   M . D .
Author of
Healing Yourself: A Step-by-Step Program for Better Health Through Imagery

Growing Older

Feeling Better

In Body, Mind & Spirit

Mary Dale Scheller, M.S.W.

BULL PUBLISHING COMPANY
PALO ALTO, CALIFORNIA

❧

Copyright 1993 Mary Dale Scheller
Bull Publishing Company
P.O. Box 208
Palo Alto, California 94302-0208
(415) 322-2855

ISBN 0-923521-22-4

Printed in the United States

Library of Congress Cataloging-in-Publication Data
Scheller, Mary Dale, 1942
Growing older, feeling better : in body, mind & spirit / by Mary Dale Scheller.
p. cm.
Includes bibliographical references and index.
ISBN 0-923521-22-4 : $12.95
1. Aged—Health and hygiene. I. Title.
RA777.6.S34 1992
613.0438—de 20   92-8648
CIP

Distributed to the trade by:
Publishers Group West
4065 Hollis Street
Emeryville, CA 94608

Cover and Interior Design: Robert Steven Pawlak Design
Cover Logo: Victoria Forrester
Back Cover Photo: Margaret Coder
Production Manager: Helen O'Donnell
Illustrations: Ken Miller and Michele Elliott
Interior Photographer: Beau Bonneau
Assistant to Photographer: John Barber
Photo Shoot Coordinator: Michele Elliott
Compositor: The Cowans
Printer: Bookcrafters, Inc.

This book is dedicated to:

Ched and Jay Scheller

who have helped me age
with a joyful spirit
and

T'Kope

whose Samoyed
smile opens my heart.

C O N T E N T S

•

ACKNOWLEDGMENTS

My deepest gratitude and appreciation is expressed to all those who have helped with the writing and publishing of this book. My special thanks goes:

*To the students from my **Health and Wholeness** classes* who provided the inspiration and encouragement for me to put our group experiences into print and to *Jack Harrington* who gave me the opportunity to teach.

*To the research participants of the **Ornish Heart Study*** who committed themselves to scientifically demonstrating that healthy lifestyle changes can reverse the effects of disease.

To Mary Patchen O'Day who introduced me to the field of gerontology through her instruction *and* her example.

*To all my instructors at the **Integral Yoga Institute** and the **Acupressure Institute of America*** for teaching me Eastern forms of healing.

To David Bull and his associates who know how to make the process of publishing a healthy and enjoyable pursuit.

To the reviewers who gave their time to improving my material. In particular, I would like to acknowledge: *Terri Merritt, MS; Judith Faye, MS, RD; Lilias Folan; Michael Reed Gach; Ping Lee; Swami Prakasanada; Swami Ramananda; James P. Scheller MD; Martin L. Rossman, MD;* and *Dean Ornish, MD.*

To my friends and family who continue to stick by me even when they find me plugged to my computer.

To Jim Scheller, my first reader, medical consultant and best friend.

As it is not proper to cure the eyes without the head,
nor the head without the body, so neither is it proper to
cure the body without the soul.

S O C R A T E S

The reason why the cure of so many diseases is
unknown to the physicians of Hellen is because they
are ignorant of the whole . . . For the part can never be
well unless the whole is well . . . For this is the great
error of our day that physicians separate body, mind
and soul.

P L A T O

INTRODUCTION

---

*I*MAGINE YOURSELF feeling full of energy, having more control of your body and emotions, smiling, laughing, feeling more at peace with yourself and others.

For the past few years I've witnessed people changing their lives for the better, at the same time that I've witnessed my own life changing and improving. Here are examples from two of my students.

I had a stroke in 1979, shortly after my retirement. Did all the rehab the hospital and outpatient services had to offer. But no matter what I did I seemed to have reached a plateau. My doctors had given up on me. My physical therapists said I had gone as far as I could go. Worse yet, I'd given up on myself. After Mary Dale's first health class, I regained what I'd lost these past ten years—hope! . . . And although I knew I could not change the brain damage resulting from the stroke, I

*learned new ways to deal with it. And I also changed my
attitude about it all.*

☙

*I have severe arthritis and I'm in pain most all the
time. My daughter read about the class in the paper and
made me go. In fact she had to pick me up and drag me
there. Reluctantly I participated. I just didn't feel well
enough to leave my own house . . . Remarkedly I began
to feel better. The gentle exercises and acupressure
helped my pain. And one day I did what I hadn't done in
five years—I squatted down and got a pan out of my
bottom kitchen cabinet. And I did it before I fully knew
what I'd done . . . My life continues to provide little miracles. With more flexibility in my hips and strength in
my legs, I can now get safely in and out of my bathtub.
Now to many of you that might not seem like a miracle.
But to an eighty year old woman, well, I felt I'd given up
bubble-baths for life!*

By the printing of this book I will have taught over
1,000 people 60 years of age and older the principles of
medical self-care. Some of the people were in excellent
health. They just wanted to have some fun staying that
way. But I also taught very courageous students learning
new ways to deal with the effects of Parkinson's Disease,
AIDS, emphysema, blindness. Some of my students
jogged into class, others came with canes and in wheelchairs. I learned from them all.

During this time I also taught heart patients for the Preventive Medicine Research Institute. Using a medically-
approved research protocol, we were trying to determine

whether comprehensive lifestyle changes (without the use of cholesterol-lowering drugs) could begin to reverse coronary atherosclerosis after only one year.

The regimen included a strict vegetarian diet, daily stress management, aerobic exercise, and twice weekly group therapy/discussions (much of the information and many of the practices set forth in this book). Upon entry into the study the 48 patients (ranging from 34-74) had at least 40% blockage in one or more vessels, with a coronary blood flow reserve less than 3.0. In other words, these were very sick people, most eligible for by-pass surgery.

The medical staff hypothesized that the younger patients and the ones with the smallest blockages would make the most improvements. The results of the first year showed this was not the case.

Adherence to the lifestyle program (regardless of age or severity of disease) was the indicator most significantly correlated with the degree of change in coronary artery disease. In other words, the more the patients followed the self-care practices, the more reversal of the blockages. And as a gerontologist I am especially pleased to tell you that the oldest patient (age 74) and the patient with the most severe coronary artery blockages were the ones who showed the greatest disease reversal. *They also devoted the most time to the program practices each day.*

GROWING OLDER, FEELING BETTER
In Body, Mind and Spirit

The health education curriculum I developed grew out of my own life journey—what had worked for me and what I'd learned from my older students and my heart patients as we traveled together. It also grew out of my firm conviction that we *can* improve the quality of our life, at any age and regardless of the severity of our problems.

So you could say I put together a class about things I wanted to learn, health practices I needed to follow. And I wanted to do this with other people who believed they, too, could feel better while growing older.

Most important, I wanted to explore not only physical health, but mental and spiritual health as well. For these reasons the lessons are perhaps more inclusive than the typical "stretch and bend" approach to health. And my students have aptly entitled this undertaking as one of "health and wholeness."

"HEALTH AND WHOLENESS"
A Five-Point Program

The components, however, are very simple. It is a five-point program for health which includes: deep three-part breathing; gentle exercise; proper nutrition and hydration (fluid maintenance with water); daily deep relaxation and acupressure techniques; regular meditations with positive visualizations. In the following chapters I'll explain each part and how each one works with the others to provide a comprehensive approach to health.

THE WISDOM OF THE AGES
BLENDED WITH MODERN MEDICAL SCIENCE

The teachings in each section are for the most part ancient knowledge derived form yoga therapy and Chinese medicine. They have held up for centuries and been passed down from generation to generation to the present day.

In recent years, these practices have also held up under Western scientific scrutiny. In fact, most schools of medicine have behavioral medicine and preventive medicine departments that now study these ancient teachings in ways consistent with modern medical practice.

With advanced technology they can now measure precisely the way our bodies react while doing these practices—the change in our brain waves, the galvanic skin response, our respiration and heart rates, our blood pressure, our antibody levels. What our ancestors knew intuitively, we can now measure scientifically.

For these reasons I like to think of the following curriculum as a health promotion program for older adults that blends the wisdom of the ages with medical science.

THE HEALTHY DIRECTION

To help you get as much as possible from the material, after each chapter I'll encourage you to make a goal for following the practices you will be learning. And I'll ask you to chart your progress each week, so that over time you will see how you are integrating the *Health and Wholeness* concepts into your life.

Your goal can be to make a small change (e.g., drinking one more glass of water a day, or taking three deep breaths before breakfast). Or it can be a comprehensive commitment like the heart patients I quoted earlier were willing to make. For an optimal wellness program this would mean a daily routine of: 3 minutes of deep breathing, 20 minutes of stretching, 30 minutes of endurance (aerobic) exercise, 15 minutes of deep relaxation, 15 minutes of meditation, 5 minutes of positive imagery, and 2 minutes of acupressure—plus a healthy diet with plenty of water.

But don't get overwhelmed. In this program it's not so important how many changes you're willing to make at once. What's important is the direction you're going.

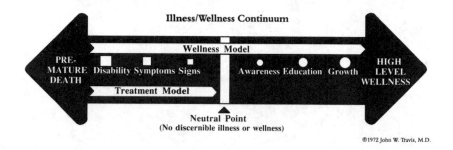

We are all at some point on our own Illness/Wellness Continuum.

At one extreme is high-level wellness. At the other is premature death. Most of us are somewhere in-between.

Dr. John Travis of Wellness Associates near Ukiah, California, shows us through his model that there are many levels of wellness, much of it accomplished through our own efforts of awareness, education and growth. He advises us to get treatment when we are ill, but urges us to move beyond our neutral point of health toward feelings of more high-level wellness.

Take some time to assess where you are on Dr. Travis's continuum. Now look at the decisions you may well have made today: *Should I eat this chocolate cake? . . . Don't have time for exercies this morning. . . . Time for me to take three deep breaths.* These moment-to-moment decisions can greatly affect your position on this chart.

Yet the discipline required to move toward greater wellness can be difficult, and the experience can be lonely. So those of us interested in *Health and Wholeness* have found ways to make our efforts fun and our goals realistically achievable. We travel together. Hope you'll come along.

PART ONE

❧

STRESS WITHOUT DISTRESS; COMFORT WITHOUT DISCOMFORT:
How to Get Started

———————————————— ❧ ————————————————

MY HUSBAND likes to tell people I teach health promotion to older people by day, stress reduction to heart patients by night, and it's all really yoga.

To some extent that's true. If you boil all healthy practices down to their early derivatives, you will find in each one some form of these ancient healing practices: body stretches, deep breathing, deep relaxation, meditation, imagery and visualization, and proper nutrition.

Both yoga and Chinese medicine deal with health and wholeness as concepts *and* as treatment modalities. They believe that the human organism is innately aware of wholeness. And no matter how our bodies have been damaged or abused, all one must do (practitioner or patient) is bring the energy back into balance.

Traditional Eastern medicine has not been so interested in relieving physical symptoms, as in keeping the body in its natural state of peace and harmony. Western medicine follows another track. It works to remove or relieve the symptoms. With this approach, it is believed the organism will heal itself.

Both approaches can work, depending on the philosophy of the doctor, the belief system of the patient, and a particular patient's body and how it best responds to treatment. What they have in common is at different levels; but to various degrees they both work at relieving stress.

Let's look at this philosophy from the Western perspective. Dr. Herbert Benson of the Harvard Medical School informs us that 75–80% of all our present-day illnesses are caused by stress. And of the 20–25% remaining disease states, he believes they can definitely become worsened through stress. It's simple: Remove the discomfort, you remove the stress, the patient gets better.

But if this is true, what about preventing stress reactions in the body to begin with? The Eastern perspective would concentrate on this. In fact in ancient China you made visits to your doctor every season, but you paid him *only* when you stayed well. That's what his work was supposed to do.

How did he do this? Mainly he taught you how to keep your body as stress-resistant as possible.

THE STRESS RESPONSE

Yet our response to stress is not necessarily harmful. It is natural, and can be physiologically useful when it helps us either to fight or run away during a crisis. During this "fight or flight response" our bodies usually respond as follows:

- Our heart beats faster

- Our blood pressure increases

- Our respiration rate increases

- Our muscles tense ready for action

- Our digestion slows down and blood flows to our muscles instead

- We perspire as our blood flows rapidly through the body

- Our pupils dilate so we can see better

- Our hearing becomes more acute

This is part of a protective mechanism that works in our favor during acute episodes of stress. But when our body responds chronically in this manner, whether there is a real crisis or not, it can wear itself down. It's like a motor revved up with no place to go. So we develop ulcers, headaches, backaches, arthritis, heart ailments, and a host of other health problems. This accelerated wearing down of our body organs and systems is what causes pathological aging, even premature death.

STRESS MANAGEMENT

We can handle on-going stress at different levels. At the external level, we can try to change our environment. When possible, we can avoid places that make us tense, people who make us cry. We can also try to eliminate the demands placed on us by others. Some of us use assertive communication. Others join labor unions. There are many ways.

But, sometimes, no matter what we do we simply do not have the influence to change external conditions. Then we need other strategies as well.

Here's what one of my heart patients learned: "I used to think it was all *their* fault—'if only my wife would shape up, if only the politicians would do their jobs,' then I could be well . . . People outside of me were upsetting me. *They* were causing my disease."

But now he explains it this way. "Now I know my own responsibility. Nobody can dictate how I react to stress. It's my choice now, whether to stay angry or whether to get well."

By doing the practices set forth in this book, the heart patients and my older students joined me in discovering that when we had no control over stressful conditions outside ourselves, we could still maintain internal control over our reactions to them. We could reduce stress by learning new ways to react to it. And we found this often had a lot to do with our perception.

PERCEPTION AND OUR STRESS RESPONSE

Just think about how you might respond to the following situation. You're driving along at the designated speed limit, but the car in front of you is going too slow. How would you respond if:

1. A stranger in the car ahead of you was *suspiciously* checking out your home?

2. A young person was, perhaps, taking driver's education?

3. A friend was slowing down, maybe to say hello?

In each case the circumstance would be the same, the car was going too slow. But your reaction to the situation would vary, I'm sure, based on how you perceived the incident.

The practices in this book help keep our bodies and minds in the most healthy and balanced state during relaxful times, such as when seeing a friend. But they also bring us back into a relaxed and healthy state when we experience inconvenience or perceive ourselves as threatened.

My yoga teacher relates the mind under stress to water moving with gravity. "If you don't do anything to change its course," he assures us, "it will naturally go downhill."

The techniques in this book give your body and mind a choice. Without ever having to control the external event, you can always have control over your reaction to it. You can change your stress response into a relaxation response. And you can learn to experience stress without distress.

COMFORT WITHOUT DISCOMFORT

The learning process itself can create distress for many of us, even those of us learning stress reduction techniques. I'm always cautioning new students not to *increase* their stress while learning how to *reduce* it. One way to accomplish this is through the concept of the "Inner Teacher."

Stay aware of your own body while doing all of the practices. If at any time you feel any discomfort or distress, that is your "Inner Teacher's" signal to slow down or completely stop the activity.

If you listen and follow your "Inner Teacher's" advice, you'll always do exactly what is right for you at that particular moment. And you'll never hurt yourself. Some of my students call it the "Whisper of Health."

A rule of thumb: It's not so much how far you can stretch or how much you can learn, but how relaxed you can remain. That's what's important during every activity in this book.

THE TRAVEL PLAN

Using a car for an analogy again, I'll lay out our travel plans. Consider that you had the most expensive, perfectly equipped automobile on the market today—a silver Mercedes, a red Ferrari, a Cadillac Seville. Take your pick.

If you didn't give it proper maintenance, no matter how well built it was or flashy it looked, eventually it just wouldn't run. Consider the exercise and stretching components of the program as our tune-ups, our maintenance program.

Now if our car were perfectly maintained, but we failed to fill it with gas or used cheap gasoline, we couldn't go very far or for very long. Consider the deep-breathing (oxygen) and the nutrition and water our fuel.

However, even if we had a properly maintained car full of gas, but we didn't know where we wanted to go or how to get there, we could be driving around aimlessly. Or we would be so depressed or frustrated we'd never venture out of our driveway at all. Meditation and visualization practices help us focus our minds and find our direction.

And the deep relaxation keeps us calm as we drive, so that no external stressors can adversely affect our finely-tuned system.

FURTHER READING

BENSON, Herbert. *The Relaxation Response.* New York: William Morrow and Co., Inc., 1975.

BORYSENKO, Joan. *Minding the Body, Mending the Mind.* Reading, MA: Addison Wesley Publishing Co., 1987.

JAFFE, Dennis T. *Healing from Within: Psychological Techniques to Help the Mind Heal the Body.* New York: Simon and Schuster, Inc., rev. ed., 1986.

KEMPER, Donald W., E. Judith Deneen and James V. Giuffre. *Growing Younger Handbook.* Boise, ID: A Healthwise Publication, 3rd ed., 1987.

SELYE, Hans, *Stress Without Distress.* New York: J. P. Lippincott, 1974.

THE
FIVE-PART
PROGRAM
FOR HEALTH

POINT ONE

DEEP BREATHING:
How Did We Live Without It?

Life is in the breath,
Therefore he who only half breathes,
Half lives.
YOGA PROVERB

All things are backed by the Shade
(yin)
And faced by the Light
(yang)
And harmonized by the immaterial Breath
(ch'i.)
TAO TE CHING
Chapter XLII

In with the good air, out with the bad.
WESTERN MEDICINE SAYING

LESSON ONE
Deep Three-Part Breathing

If I could teach only one health practice, it would be deep breathing. Deep three-part breathing can be done by anybody at any time. It brings energy into your body, when you're feeling tired. It reduces tension, when you're feeling anxious or in pain. You can do it sitting, standing, lying down. It requires no special equipment, no exercise attire. No matter how sick or how well you are, you can practice breathing deeply.

It is also the quickest way to bring yourself into the body/mind/spirit connection.

PHYSICAL LEVEL

At a physical level there are many benefits, recognized by both Western and Eastern concepts of medicine.

Deep breathing brings in 7 times more oxygen than our normal, shallow breathing. Oxygen is needed to nourish the cells, and bring us energy and vitality. We know how important food and water are for life. But to stay alive doctors tell us we can go up to 40 days without food, 4 days without water. Yet we can go only 4 minutes without oxygen before we experience brain damage.

With this practice *you also release more carbon dioxide*, getting rid of waste products and toxins in the system. Doctors tell us to go to bed and drink water, when we are sick. Yogis believe you should go to bed, drink water, and lengthen your exhalations.

11

When you deep breathe, *you must exercise and therefore strengthen many muscles in the body*—the abdominal recti muscles (tummy muscles), the diaphragm (the muscle that separates our respiratory system from our digestive one), the intercostals (between the ribs), the pectoral, latissimus, and trapezius muscles (which all help expand, contract, lift and lower the upper chest).

Joanie Greggains, a San Francisco T.V. fitness personality, recommends deep breathing as the best possible exercise for tightening abdominal muscles. Opera singers and yogis all develop strong chest muscles from the regular practice of proper breathing.

You increase metabolic function. Many people, without even planning it, begin to lose weight or stop smoking after beginning a daily breathing practice. As our metabolic system begins to operate optimally we not only feel better, we tend to lose our craving for unhealthy substances.

As soon as deep breathing begins, *receptors in the lungs immediately release tension in muscle groups throughout the body.* Tense muscles are painful. When the muscles are relaxed, this pain is reduced or eliminated. So when someone is suffering from chronic pain, I begin them immediately on a breathing regimen.

By expanding and contracting these muscles, you send *a gentle massage to many organs*—the heart, the liver, the pancreas, the stomach, the spleen, small and large intestine, and other abdominal organs. Yogis have been recommending deep breathing as a treatment for heart ailments for centuries. Not only does it lower blood pressure, and lower the respiration and heart rates, it massages the heart as well.

You see, when the abdominal muscles expand, the diaphragm pulls down. The pericardial sac (which surrounds the heart) is attached to the diaphragm. And this sac gives a gentle stimulation to the cardiac muscles and arteries. The movement of the diaphragm and other muscles work on additional organs in similar ways.

MENTAL AND EMOTIONAL LEVELS

The brain and nervous system get more oxygen. I always recommend to my college-age sons that when taking exams, they go to class early, sit still and deep breathe. Now this won't help if they haven't studied. But if the information is already in the brain, deep breathing reduces test anxiety and allows for better recall. When my older students complain of memory problems, one thing I have them do is begin to deepen their breathing during some part of the day.

If you looked at a cross-section of the nose, you'd notice clearly the close proximity of the nasal passage to the brain. Yoga experts recognize that nasal breathing stimulates the olfactory nerve and this nerve provides the direct link to the brain. Therefore, yoga practitioners believe that *nasal breathing stimulates and tones the brain and nervous system.*

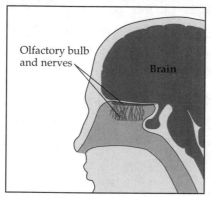
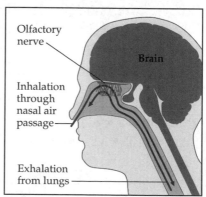

Although Western medicine has lagged far behind in its research on the importance of breathing and health, there have been advances in recent years. All childbirth training relies on some form of yogic breathing. The breathing helps reduce pain and to support the birthing process. Similarly, biofeedback training usually includes some type of breathing to reduce stress.

The Salk Institute for Biological Studies in San Diego has gone further. Researchers there have studied the effect of deep breathing (using one nostril at a time) on the treatment of depression and schizophrenia. The nose, (often viewed by Western physicians as a fixture merely for inhaling and exhaling air, or an olfactory device simply for detecting odors), now is being looked at more closely. The Salk Institute is trying to measure what the yogis have always known, that *the respiratory system is an intricate device for actively altering the state of mind, and even for treating complicated mental and emotional disorders.*

In fact, yogic feats involving the control of the involuntary systems of the body are developed first through the yogic control of the breath. The respiratory system is the only system in the body that is both voluntary and involuntary. We don't have to think about breathing and we still breathe. On the other hand we can learn to regulate the breath, to breathe more deeply, to breathe in specified rhythms, or at certain intervals, with specific nostrils.

With knowledge and practice the yogis know that to gain more conscious control of our breathing, *we can eventually gain conscious control over other unconscious aspects of our life.*

14

But we don't have to accomplish extraordinary feats. By working with the breath we can *affect our everyday emotional state.*

Notice how you breathe when angry, when afraid, depressed. If you exaggerate these breathing patterns, you can intensify these feelings and these emotional states. Now, notice how you breathe when happy and at peace. The quickest way to move yourself out of either an anxious or a depressed state is to deepen your breathing pattern. The emotions will follow how you breathe. Try it.

THE SPIRITUAL LEVEL

Almost all spiritual teachers, especially Eastern ones, encourage breath work to *deepen spiritual development.* The word "inspire" comes from the Latin derivative which means to be filled with the breath of gods. Hildegard of Bingen, a spiritual mystic who lived in Europe eight centuries ago, defined prayer as "breathing in and breathing out the one breath of the universe."

Present Judeo-Christian practices, however, seem to have lost track of these teachings. Yet if you go back to the original Aramaic translations, breath work is a central part of the scriptural teachings.

For example, Neil Douglas-Klotz in his book, *Prayers of the Cosmos,* has translated several passages from the *Bible* into the native language that Jesus spoke. Here are some of his translations.

From the Lord's Prayer:

KING JAMES VERSION
Our Father which art in heaven. Hallowed be thy name. Thy kingdom come. Thy will be done in earth, as it is in heaven . . .

ARAMAIC TRANSLATION
O Birther! Father-Mother of the Cosmos, you create all that moves in light. O Thou! The Breathing Life of all . . . Respiration of all worlds, we hear you breathing—in and out—in silence . . .

From the Beatitudes:

KING JAMES VERSION
Blessed are the poor in spirit: for theirs is the kingdom of heaven . . .

ARAMAIC TRANSLATION
Happy and aligned with the One are those who find their home in the breathing; to them belong the inner kingdom and queendom of heaven. Blessed are those who are refined in breath; they shall find their ruling principles and ideals guided by God's light . . .

BREATHING AS A SPIRITUAL PRACTICE

But how can *we* apply deep breathing at a spiritual level? One simple way to bring deep breathing into our daily life is to teach a friend who is upset how to reduce her stress. In so doing we *can connect with her at a very deep level.*

Another way is to teach deep breathing to hospitalized friends, if they are ready and interested. The exhalations will expel any residue of anesthesia still left in the lungs. They will also reduce stress and pain. The inhalations will bring energy and vitality into their systems.

You don't necessarily have to teach a great deal. When teaching in convalescent hospitals, I don't go into full breathing instructions. I just have the residents raise their arms high over their heads on the inhalation, and then bend forward on the exhalation. These movements of themselves cause the lungs to increase their expansions and contractions.

We've mentioned breathing during childbirth, but very few people recognize the importance of breathing during the dying process. When I am in the presence of a person who is very ill and dying, I rarely talk; instead I go into deep three-part breathing on my own. I don't know exactly what happens, but there is an effect on the other people who are present. Perhaps as we *reduce our stress, those around us can relax and let go.*

When my father was in a coma and dying, I breathed with him. Whenever he went into a Cheyne-Stokes breathing pattern (a gasping breath, typical of dying patients), my breathing would bring him into a state of calmness. Maybe it was coincidental. But maybe not.

Anya Goos-Graber in her book, *Deathing: An Intelligent Alternative for the Final Moments of Life,* instructs readers how to coach dying patients to let go with their breath. Maybe we do more to *share energy with others* than we fully understand.

Start by incorporating deep breathing into your personal worship. Breathe before you pray. Breathe as part of your daily meditation. Notice what happens if you begin to deep breathe as a part of your religious service. The effects can be very powerful.

EXERCISE 1–1
DEEP THREE-PART BREATHING: THE PRACTICE

To learn deep three-part breathing, I've found it often useful to isolate the steps into three stages.

BEGINNING POSITION: Sit up straight, with the spine erect, shoulders back, and head centered. Chin is parallel to the floor.

FIRST STAGE BREATHING

 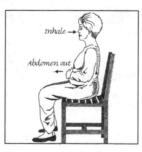 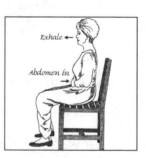

| *Beginning Position* | *Step 2* | *Step 3* |

1. Exhale fully.

2. Inhale and allow the abdominal muscles to expand like a balloon filling up with air. (You may want to place your hand on your abdomen and feel the muscles move out.) (See Step 2 diagram.)

3. Exhale and pull the abdomen in toward the spine. (Feel the abdominal muscles tighten, squeezing out more air from the lungs.) (See Step 3 diagram.)

19

4. Continue for about 5 or 6 breaths at a rhythm comfortable to you. (Be sure the abdomen goes out on the inhalation, in on the exhalation.)

5. On the next exhalation, relax. (You have just completed the first stage of this breathing practice.)

SECOND STAGE BREATHING

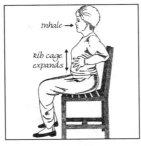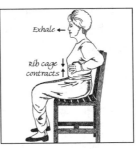

Step 8   *Step 9*

6. To begin the second part, first exhale fully.

7. Inhale and feel the abdomen expand. (As in #2.)

8. Now bring the breath to the area of your rib cage and feel it expand. (You can place your hands along the rib cage and feel the muscles between the ribs widen.) (See Step 8 diagram.)

9. On the exhalation, feel these muscles contract. (See Step 9 diagram.)

10. Now pull in the abdomen toward the spine. (As in #3.)

11. Continue for about 5 or 6 breaths at your own rate and rhythm. (You are doing two-part breathing.)

12. On the next exhalation, relax the breath.

DEEP THREE-PART BREATHING

Step 16   *Step 17*

13. Now the complete practice. Exhale fully.

14. Inhale and allow the abdominal muscles to expand. (As in #2.)

15. Allow the intercostal muscles between the ribs to expand. (As in #8.)

16. Allow the collarbones to rise slightly. (You may want to place your hands on the collarbones to feel them rise.) (See Step 16 diagram.)

17. On the exhalation, the collarbones lower slightly and the upper chest contracts. (See Step 17 diagram.)

18. The lower chest contracts. (As in #9.)

19. The abdomen pulls in. (As in #3.)

20. Continue from one to three minutes at your own rate and rhythm. (This is deep three-part breathing.)

21. To end the practice, exhale fully and relax.

Now that you have mastered the three stages, you can begin at Step #13 and proceed to #21 for an integrated practice. Your hands can remain on your lap and you may want to close your eyes.

DEEP THREE-PART BREATHING:
"AEROBIC" EXERCISE

Dr. Sandra McLanahan at the Integral Health Clinic in Charlottesville, Virignia measured the lung capacity of patients after three activities. After normal, shallow breathing, her patients were taking in 500 cc of air with each breath; after 15 minutes of aerobic exercise they were taking in 700 cc of air; and after three minutes of deep three-part breathing they were taking in 3200 cc of air.

This is why some yoga practitioners say deep three-part breathing is the best "aerobic" exercise we can do. Aerobic, in this case, means with oxygen.

IS PROPER BREATHING
REALLY SO IMPORTANT?

One of my students voiced a typical reaction: "I can't believe that after 84 years, I'm being told I'm not breathing correctly."

If we're alive, I often explain, we're using some part of our lungs to breathe. If we're not comfortable with deep three-part breathing, we're probably not using our vital lung capacity.

Here's an exercise to find out what parts of your lungs you are using and what your particular breathing pattern may be doing for you.

EXERCISE 1–2
A BREATHING DEMONSTRATION

THE ABDOMINAL BREATHER

1. Do only the first stage breathing. (Steps # 1–4 on page 19.)

2. Stand up and exaggerate this breathing pattern.

3. Now walk around the room and talk socially to other people in the room. "Hello, how are you?" "Fine, thank you." Do this for approximately five minutes, remembering to use the lower area of your lungs predominately to breathe.

Concentrated
Abdominal Breathing

4. Bring your breath back to normal. Take a few moments to listen to your body.

- What did that feel like to you? Was it natural or unnatural? Comfortable? Uncomfortable?

- What did you notice in your body? Any areas of tightness or stress? What areas of the body specifically?

- What physical problems do you think you might have or develop if you used only your abdominal muscles to breathe? (Or in the next example your chest muscles?)

- What kind of personality do you think you might develop?

THE CHEST BREATHER

1. Bring your breath to the upper area of your lungs and breathe predominately in that area. (Steps # 16 & 17 on page 21.)

2. Stand up and walk around greeting the other people in the room. Remember to keep your breathing as much in the upper lung segments as possible for five minutes or so.

Concentrated
Chest Breathing

3. Bring your breath back to normal and ask yourself the same questions you asked in the previous exercise, but this time focusing on the effect of chest breathing and the use of chest muscles.

MAKING DEEP BREATHING A
PART OF DAILY LIFE

The purpose of these exercises is to determine the segment of your lungs you tend to use for your normal, shallow breathing. Changing your breathing habits begins by identifying the area of the lungs you unconsciously use for breathing. Then, for greater health, you can gradually and consciously begin to enlarge this area of space.

The purpose of this class is not simply to stay alive. What we're striving for is to be more *fully alive.* There are many ways to become healthier, but the most effective and quickest way I've found is to begin with finding time each day to do some deep three-part breathing.

Our breathing pattern, whether we are aware of it or not, establishes our energy flow. Our energy flow affects our body, our emotions, our personality, even our character. Therefore, when we work with our breath we can change our life enormously.

Some people immediately improve their posture and their body appearance. Some with time report seeing colors more vividly, hearing better, remembering more. Many people find the practice helps them go to sleep more quickly. Others find it keeps them generally feeling better throughout the day. For most of us, it helps us become more conscious.

RECOMMENDED BREATHING PROGRAM
FOR HEALTH

FOR OPTIMAL HEALTH

1. At least 3 minutes a day of deep three-part breathing with the mind fully focused on the breath.

TO FEEL BETTER

1. Any time you are feeling stressed (changing the stress response into the relaxation response).

2. Any time you are unable to sleep.

3. Any time you are waiting in line, stuck in traffic, placed on telephone hold, sitting in a doctor's office.

PRECAUTIONS

If you feel lightheaded or dizzy, bring your breath back to your normal breathing rhythm. Relax. These signals are your "Inner Teacher" letting you know your brain and nervous system are just not quite ready for so much intake of oxygen and/or so much release of carbon dioxide. Take your time and gradually increase your breathing time to your personal comfort level.

PERSONAL BREATHING GOAL

I will practice deep-three-part breathing for _____ minutes per day for _____ weeks and notice how I feel.

PROGRESS REPORT

Date

_____

What Done

_____

_____

_____

_____

Improvements Noticed

_____

_____

_____

_____

_____

_____

_____

Reported to Whom

_____

28

PART TWO

FURTHER READING

DOUGLAS-KLOTZ, Neil. *Prayers of the Cosmos: Meditations on the Aramaic Words of Jesus.* San Francisco: Harper and Row, 1990.

DYCHTWALD, Kenneth. *Bodymind.* New York: Pantheon Books, 1977.

FOOS-GRABER, Anya. *Deathing: An Intelligent Alternative for the Final Moments of Life.* Reading, MA: Addison-Wesley Publishing Co., 1984.

IYENGAR, B.K.S. *Light on Pranayama.* New York: Schocken Books, 1966.

RAMA, S., Rudolph Ballentine and Alan Hymes. *Science of Breath: A Practical Guide.* Honesdale, PA: Himalayan International Institute, 3rd ed., 1981.

SATCHIDANANDA, Sri Swami. *Integral Hatha Yoga.* New York: Holt, Rinehart and Winston, 1970.

SHANNAHOFF-KHALSA, David. *Breathing, Mind and Metabolism.* The Salk Institute for Biological Studies: P.O. Box 85800, San Diego, CA., 92138. (Document)

POINT TWO

Stretching and Moving:
How the Body Wants to Move and Deserves to Feel

At birth, man is born gentle and weak
At death, he is hard and stiff,
At birth, a plant is tender with sap
At death, it is withered and dry
Therefore: the flexible are the disciples of the living
the stiff are the disciples of death.

TAO TE CHING

What you cannot learn in the body,
you can learn no where else.

BHAGAVAD GITA

Use it or lose it.

CONTEMPORARY WESTERN SAYING

The body is a marvelous machine, able to accomplish amazing feats. But to stay in working order, its parts must be moved, its joints must be oiled, and its pipes must be cleaned.

Many health problems are attributed to growing old:

- stiff and inflamed joints
- high blood pressure
- lower back problems
- shortness of breath
- indigestion
- overweight
- constipation
- poor sleep habits
- poor balance
- reduced energy

Through a gentle stretching and moving program *Health and Wholeness* students are astonished by how quickly they feel better, and how with regular practice, many of these symptoms eventually begin to disappear. Could it be that many of the problems associated with aging are merely the effects of poor health habits, especially inactivity? Would you be interested in experimenting with your own health problems, to see how much better you too, can feel?

DIFFERENT TYPES OF EXERCISE

There are different types of exercises for the body. Strengthening and endurance (dynamic) exercises strengthen the muscles, heart, lungs, and circulatory system. Flexibility exercises keep the muscles long and pliable.

The strengthening/endurance exercises help you remain active for longer periods of time. The endurance exercises are often referred to as aerobic exercise, which implies that you are allowing for an adequate supply of oxygen to be available for your working muscles. With this type of exercise you develop your cardiac muscles and lung capacity. Strengthening exercises develop most of your skeletal muscles.

As you develop skeletal muscles, you also can maintain and/or build bone density. You can see how, when practiced in a prudent and regular manner, these exercises can help prevent or lessen the effects of problems due to arthritis, cardiovascular disease, osteoporosis and other illnesses associated with growing older.

Muscles are strengthened primarily through exercises that contract them. But when muscles are subjected only to strengthening exercises, without a flexibility program, they will eventually shorten and become too tight.

As we age, our muscles typically shorten and the tissues around our joints thicken. If we do not counter this aging process, we will soon find our ability to reach, to turn, and move in all directions severely impaired. Just as strengthening exercises work primarily on the contraction principle, the flexibility exercises work primarily on the expansion principle of the body.

THE EASTERN APPROACH

Chinese and yogic methods of therapy both emphasize a gentle form of stretching to increase flexibility. The ancient teachings rarely, if ever, mention the need for the strengthening and endurance movements. The main reason, I believe, is that in olden times people *had* to perform strengthening exercise to survive. They didn't choose whether to walk or ride to the village, they walked. When they plowed the fields, they had no tractors. They were forced to use their bodies continuously in their daily lives, whether they liked it or not.

The ancient teachings did recognize how the muscles shortened and tissues hardened with age. Whether people worked the body vigorously or lay sick in bed, they knew their bodies would automatically move into a more contracted state. (This is why people in comas must be regularly stretched or their bodies will contracted into a tight fetal position.)

To work against this contraction process, they encouraged movements focused on stretching and opening the body (the expansion principle), not those that tightened and closed it down. And although modern-day yoga moves the body in all directions, generally more emphasis is given to expansion poses than to poses that strengthen muscles or build endurance.

Another important point in both Chinese and yogic practices is that students must keep an inward focus. This is believed to be necessary in order to engage the body and mind at subtle energy levels (that relax rather than tax the system).

This is next to impossible with most aerobic activity. Just to avoid collision while walking, swimming, running, or engaging in any other forward-moving activity, participants must keep an outward focus. To keep both an inward and outward focus at the same time is considered difficult, if not impossible by the yogis.

THE HEALTH AND WHOLENESS APPROACH

The *Health and Wholeness* program strives to bring together the best from Eastern and Western thought. Because most of us tend to lead sedentary lives, we believe some sort of strengthening and endurance program (dynamic exercise) is necessary, especially as we age.

THE TENDENCY TO GAIN FAT

There is another important reason, according to Dr. Jack Wilmore, professor of Exercise Science at the University of Texas at Austin. After maturity (which for most people is approximately 30 years of age), unless we are physically active, we can expect to lose about $1/2$ pound of lean muscle tissue a year. In this country, most people after maturity tend not only to make up that loss, but to gain an additional pound of fat each year. So on the average, we can expect to gain a total of $1^1/2$ pounds of fat each year.

That is why by age sixty, unless we reduce considerably our caloric in-take or burn up these extra calories through exercise, we can usually expect to be substantially heavier than we were as young adults. (Although the numbers will be different with different folks, if you would like to calculate this out, you'll see we're talking about a typical sixty-year-old person having 30 pounds more over-all weight, with 45 pounds more fat.)

THE FLEXIBILITY PROGRAM FROM AN
EASTERN PERSPECTIVE

The *Health and Wholeness* program also includes a flexibility program. We, however, teach it from an Eastern perspective. By slowing down the movements and focusing

---

the mind on the body in a conscious way, we work at a deeper level than just lengthening muscles and loosening joints.

THE IMPORTANCE OF BREATHING

We do not believe any aerobic exercise program should replace a regular breathing practice. Although all the exercises in this chapter incorporate continuous, natural breathing, none should replace the need for deep three-part breathing. This we feel is the best way to maintain lung capacity and eliminate any lactic acid that may have accumulated in the muscle tissue. Specifically, to enhance the exercise program, and to prevent any muscle soreness, we recommend deep three-part breathing before and after any dynamic movements and between each stretching movement.

INWARD AND OUTWARD FOCUS

Finally, we believe it is possible to learn to focus both inwardly and outwardly, when any movement forward is done slowly enough. We introduce this practice with the "Walking Awareness Exercise," and encourage its use in the regular walking program as well.

LESSON TWO
A Flexibility Program

We've combined a set of therapeutic stretches taken from both the yogic and the Chinese traditions. Many of them have been adapted for use in Western-based stretching programs.

From a Western perspective, these are usually applied to "Warm-Up" or "Cool-Down" phases practiced before and after a more strenuous exercise program. From the Eastern perspective, they are much more. Let's take a look at them in terms of their origins.

Typically yoga is done by moving the body into a pose, holding the position a few moments, then moving back to the original starting point. Each pose is chosen for its therapeutic effect on a particular part of the body. While one holds the position, there is in effect a gentle massage of the designated body part and a slight restriction of blood flow to that particular organ, muscle, gland, or joint. When the body is released from the pose, the return of the increased blood flow provides healing energy to that area of the body.

The Chinese movements, on the other hand, are generally more fluid, providing stretching not only to the body area, but, in Chinese terms, to the energy meridians running through that area as well. (These meridians will be explained more thoroughly in the lesson on acupressure.)

Both practices focus the mind on the body. We'll discuss the additional advantages of this approach later. The immediate benefit is that the body is better able to direct blood to the parts being moved.

Both the yogic and the Chinese practices also give conscious attention to the breath. This is very important. First, it helps keep the muscle tissues relaxed while they are being stretched. Secondly, it insures that when the blood is directed to a particular part of the body, that part of the body is fully supplied with oxygen to adequately nourish its cells.

Both practices are very gentle, but don't let that fool you. They are also very powerful.

While Western approaches usually are satisfied with stretching muscles and moving joints, these stretches, when applied correctly, do much more. They benefit all the major systems—the muscular-skeletal, digestive, respiratory, circulatory, genito-urinary, and particularly the nervous system.

They also *tone* the endocrine and the immune systems. When we use the word tone, we are referring to the balancing concept mentioned earlier. That is why after doing these exercises one student may feel energized, while another may feel completely relaxed. Each person gets what his or her body needs most.

Although gentle enough even for those severely disabled, the exercises can benefit any person of any age and fitness level. In fact, the Chinese folk exercises included here have been selected from hundreds that were used therapeutically by those injured while engaging in the martial arts. Although easy to do, they are definitely not for sissies. In fact many of our major professional football teams are now incorporating some sort of yogic stretching into their conditioning routines for the muscular-skeletal effect alone.

Here is how I suggest you approach the stretching program:

1. Listen to your "Inner Teacher" and follow the "Whisper of Health." That is, at the first moment of strain, pain, dizziness or any other discomfort, stop the movement and relax.

2. Move slowly with awareness. Keep your mind focused on the area being benefited. And remember, the more slowly you can move your body, the greater the neuro-physiological effect.

3. Your breathing should be natural and through the nostrils, except for Stretches 13–15 where the exhalation is through the mouth.

The Chinese say this is to produce an "internal breath," a concept common to the Chinese breathing science called Qi Gung. Although this has no exact counterpart in our culture, students often describe their experience as the feeling of an internal massage. And this is exactly what you want. You should feel each movement, rather than just be "going through the motions." The breath will help you keep this body/mind presence.

4. Except for Stretches 16–20, I teach most of the classes sitting down in a chair. I've found that all my students can participate this way, even those in wheelchairs. However, most of the movements can also be done from a standing position as well. If you choose to stand, please have a steady chair or wall nearby for support. And only stand as long as you feel steady and balanced.

5. At the end of certain poses, I'll ask you to shake out parts of your body that may be holding tension. This is especially important in the beginning stages, since the learning itself may set us up for the stress response.

6. Take a deep three-part breath and relax between each stretch. The relaxation allows time for the body to integrate the learning from the stretch. You can also enjoy the practice more when you are able to stay completely relaxed throughout the entire program.

7. Although you can do each stretch as many times as feels good to your body, for now I recommend 3 times on each side and/or in each direction. After the learning phase, the entire routine should require no more than 15–20 minutes.

EXERCISE 2–1
THE THERAPEUTIC STRETCHES

TO STRETCH THE SPINE IN DIFFERENT DIRECTIONS
AND PREPARE THE BODY FOR
THE REST OF THE POSES

BEGINNING SITTING POSITION

Sit tall in a chair with your spine long, shoulders back, head centered. Have your hands in your lap and your feet placed evenly on the floor. This is the beginning position for all of the seated stretches. You may want to place a towel at the area of your lower back for support

OPENING
(Adaptive Yoga Pose) (Choose One Option)

1. Sun Salutation
(Option One—For People with Lower Back Difficulties)

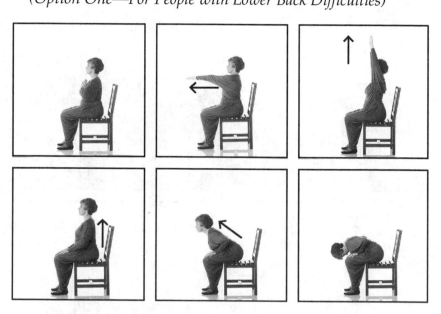

Press your palms in front of your chest with both thumbs touching your breastbone. Lock your thumbs, stretch your arms out in front of you and up over your head with fingertips to the ceiling. Stretch up and hold for a moment, then stretch your arms out as you come down parallel to your thighs. Now place your hands on the upper thighs. Lift your chin and bend forward to the area comfortable for you. (Your chest is towards or on your thighs.) Hold position for 2 or 3 breaths. (If you feel dizzy, lift your chin or come out of the pose at any time.)

To come out of the pose, press your hands against your thighs for support. Keeping your spine stretched out, return your body to an upright position. Bring your palms back in front of your chest. Exhale. Take a deep breath. Relax in the beginning position with your hands back in your lap.

1. Sun Salutation
(Option Two—For People with Strong Lower Back Muscles)

Begin with posture described in *Option One* with your palms in front of your chest. Lock your thumbs, stretch your arms out and up, stretch up tall and bend back slightly from your hips. (Do not bend your neck backwards.) Stretch up tall, lift your ribs, arms along side of your ears, and keep your spine stretched. Now fold forward until your hands come towards the floor. Relax. (If you get dizzy, lift your chin or come out of the pose.) Hold for 2 or 3 breaths.

To come out of the pose, lock your thumbs, stretch your arms out in front of you, alongside your ears and lift rib cage. Arch back slightly. Return your palms back to their beginning position in front of your chest. Exhale. Take a deep breath. Relax in the beginning position with your hands in your lap.

TO BENEFIT THE EYES

2. Eye Movements

(The goal is to stretch your eyes as far to the periphery of your field of vision as possible, without strain.) (Yoga Pose)

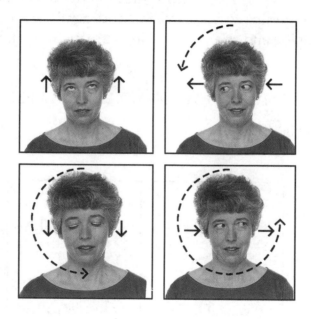

Clockwise Circles—Look up with your eyes as high as you can, and begin moving your eyes around to the right. Be sure to touch all points on the circle. You might think of the circle as a clock. Notice any numbers on this clock where your eyes want to skip or jump. Pay special attention to these points on the next rounds. Complete three full circles. When your eyes come to the top of the circle the third time, close them and relax.

Counterclockwise Circles—Repeat in a counterclockwise direction. Complete three rounds. When your eyes come to the top of the circle on the third round, close your eyes and relax.

Place your palms together and rub them until they are nice and warm. Cup your palms and place them over your eyelids with your fingertips pointed upward toward the hairline. When the heat in your palms dissipates, bring your fingertips to your eyelids and gently stroke them to the outside and relax. Take a deep breath and relax.

TO STRENGTHEN AND RELAX
TONGUE AND FACIAL MUSCLES

3. Facial Squeeze
(Yoga Pose)

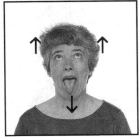

Make a tiny face, squeezing all the facial muscles together towards the point of your nose. Hold it . . . Relax. Make a very wide face, open your eyes and try to look backwards. Now open your mouth, stick out your tongue. Hold it . . . Relax. Repeat two more times. Take a deep breath and relax.

44

TO BENEFIT THE NECK MUSCLES

4. Chin to Chest
(Chinese Therapeutic Movement)

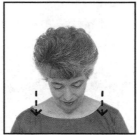

Sit tall with your neck stretched and lifted as long as possible. Now gently and slowly bring your chin to your chest. Do not force or collapse. Now gently and slowly return your chin back to its original upright position. Remember to breathe naturally throughout. (Do not tilt your head backwards, especially if you feel any dizziness or lightheadedness.) When you've completed three rounds, bring your head to center. Take a deep breath and relax.

5. Ear to Shoulder
(Chinese Therapeutic Movement)

Sit tall with your neck stretched as long as comfortable. Now lower your right ear gently towards your right shoulder. As you hold for 2 or 3 breaths, can you feel the stretch on the opposite side. Your shoulders stay even. Your neck remains still. Allow the weight of your head to do most of the stretching. Breathe. Then gently bring your head back to center. Next lower your left ear gently towards your left shoulder. Continue breathing. Now gently bring your head back to center and relax. Continue for two more rounds. Take a deep breath and relax with your hands in your lap.

6. Big Semi-Circles with the Head
(Chinese Therapeutic Movement)

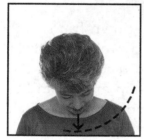
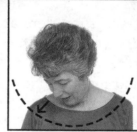

Check your posture as instructed in the first exercise, seeing that your spine is long with its natural curves, shoulders are back, and your head is centered. Moving slowly look over your left shoulder. Chin stays down as you move your head to the right. Now turn to look over your right shoulder, making a semi-circle with your head. Now move from right to left. (Do not bend neck backwards to make full circles.) Now two more times very slowly. Remember to breathe naturally. When finished, take a deep breath and relax with hands in your lap.

TO BENEFIT THE SHOULDER MUSCLES

7. Shoulder Rolls

  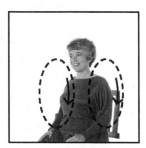

Sit tall. Spine is erect, shoulders are down from your ears, and your head is centered. Start by rolling both of your shoulders, first in a backwards direction. Feel the muscles stretching and moving. Now stop and begin the rolls in the opposite direction. Let your breath be natural. (This stretch loosens the entire shoulder girdle.) Take a deep breath and relax.

8. Chinese Shoulder Rolls
(Chinese Therapeutic Movement)

Sit tall. Start by raising your shoulders up as in the previous exercise, rolling them up to the highest point on the circle. Hold this position and then allow them to drop of their own weight. Experience the feeling of your shoulders moving up to the top of their arc and then letting go on their own. When standing, this movement works with gravity and helps us feel more grounded. Choose which method you prefer.

Move three times in both directions. Breathe. Now repeat the exercise three times in the opposite direction. Take a deep breath and relax.

TO BENEFIT THE HANDS, FINGERS, WRISTS

9. Fingers Squeeze

Extend your arms in front at shoulder height, palms down. Now slowly squeeze your fingers, making your hands into fists. Squeeze and release approximately 6 times. Now turn your palms up, and repeat approximately 6 times. Shake out your fingers. Bring them to your lap, take a deep breath and relax.

10. Soup Stirring with the Hands
(Chinese Therapeutic Movement)

Extend your arms in front at shoulder height with your palms toward the floor. Keeping your elbows straight, rotate wrists in small circles as if stirring a pot of soup. Rotate 3 times in each direction. Now pretend that the potatoes are stuck in the bottom of the pot, and begin to scrape the pot. Slowly point your fingertips toward floor, and then toward the ceiling. Repeat three times. Shake out your hands. Take a deep breath. Relax.

11. Claws/Beaks/Paws
(Chinese Therapeutic Movement)

| Tigers' Claws | Birds' Beaks | Bears' Paws |

With your arms out in front of you, spread your fingers and turn your fingers slightly inward like you were making tigers' claws. Now move your fingers together and rotate your wrist to the outside as if you are forming two birds' beaks each pointing to the outside. Now bring your fingers together into a fist, while rotating your wrist back to the original position. Imagine you are making bears' paws. Your wrists have now completed a full rotation. Repeat in the other direction. Note that you first make a claws/beaks/paws then make paws/beaks/claws. Shake out your hands, take a deep breath and relax. (Besides bringing flexibility to your fingers and wrists, this exercise stimulates the brain and nervous system as well.)

TO BENEFIT THE UPPER SPINE,
SHOULDER JOINTS, AND UPPER TORSO

12. Cobra
(Adaptive Yoga Pose)

Sit tall with your hands in your lap. Bend your elbows with your fingertips toward the ceiling and your palms facing the wall in front of you. Keep your arms close to the sides of your body. Lift your chin slightly. Slowly arch backward as slowly as possible and as far as is comfortable. Hold for approximately 2 or 3 breaths, making sure there is no pain in the upper neck. Now slowly return to starting position. Relax. Repeat twice. Remember to breathe and keep your mind focused between your shoulder blades. After the third round, take a deep breath and relax fully.

BEGINNING STANDING POSITION

The beginning for all standing poses is this: Stand tall with feet shoulder distance apart and knees slightly bent. Spine is erect, shoulders are back and head is centered. You should feel steady and well-balanced.

13. Tiger from the Heart
(Standing recommended) (Qi Gung)

Position your hands like tigers' claws as in Stretch 11. Beginning with bent elbows, extend your hands outward from your heart, circle around towards the back, rotating hands inward, and then push out from your heart again. (Arm motion is like swimming the breast stroke.) *Breathe out through your mouth* as your arms extend. Repeat twice. Shake out, take a deep breath. Relax.

14. Tiger from the Sky
(Standing recommended) (Qi Gung)

Begin with the standing position described on page 54.

Position your hands like tigers' claws again. Reach both hands up towards the sky. Bend the elbows so both hands are in front of your heart and extend them outward as in Stretch 13. *Exhale through your mouth* as arms extend. Repeat two more times. Shake out, take a deep breath. Relax.

15. Dragon from the Sky
(Standing recommended) (Qi Gung)

Begin with standing position described on page 54.

Your hands are raised to the sky. Gently shift your weight to your right foot. Now turn your palms over to face the earth and lower your arms to your right approximately waist height. Next you raise your hands to the sky, shift your weight to your left. Palms are turned toward the earth as you move them to waist height on your left. Continue, *exhaling through your mouth.* Slow, easy movements. Imagine the vastness of the dragon as it lightly touches the earth first on the right and then on the left.

TO BENEFIT LOWER SPINE, WAIST, HIPS, LOWER TORSO

16. Half Locust
(Standing required) (Adaptive Yoga Pose)

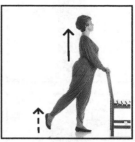

Stand behind your chair and hold on to its back for support. Lift your head and torso upward toward the ceiling. Feel the stretch in your abdominal region.

Next extend your right leg backwards and touch the floor with your toes, but as you do, continue to feel the stretch upwards toward the ceiling. *Now if you are experiencing no discomfort in the lower back,* begin to raise your right leg a few inches, keeping the spine erect. (Imagine you have a lighted candle on the top of your head, and you have to be sure the candle will not tip, as you lift your leg.) Hold approximately 2 or 3 breaths. Release and relax. Now repeat the movements extending your left leg backwards, continuing to feel the stretch upwards. Again, if lower back is comfortable, begin to raise your left leg a few inches. Hold approximately 2 or 3 breaths. Release and relax. Repeat two more times. Shake out. Take a deep breath. Relax.

17. Hip Circles
(Standing required) (Chinese Therapeutic Movement)

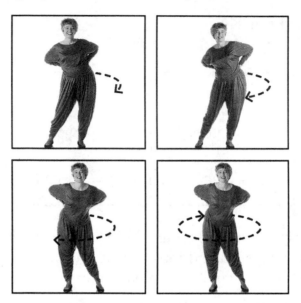

Assume beginning standing position: Feet are shoulder distance apart, knees slightly bent. Posture is erect and head is centered.

Place your hands on your lower back with fingertips toward the floor. Rotate your hips, keeping your body long and lifted as though connected by a thread to the sky. Go in both directions three times. Shake out. Take a deep breath. Relax.

18. Arm Swing

(Standing recommended) (Chinese Therapeutic Movement)

In this standing position, your feet are together. Stand tall.

Tighten your buttocks, abdominal muscles, and squeeze urinary and anal sphincters. While holding these muscles, swing your arms forward and backward for 6 counts breathing comfortably. Relax your muscles and continue to swing your arms for 6 counts. Continue the cycle two more times, remembering to breathe. Shake out. Now, take a deep breath. Relax.

TO BENEFIT THE ENTIRE SPINE

19. Luminous Egg of Breath
(Standing recommended) (Chinese Therapeutic Movement)

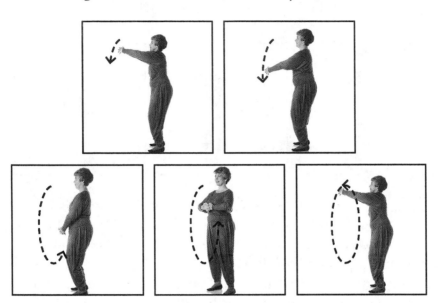

Assume original standing position: Feet shoulder distance apart, knees slightly bent, spine is erect and head is centered.

Clasp your hands together with your fingers interlaced. Palms are facing inward. Straighten your elbows and bring your hands and arms overhead. Stretch up and out with your arms as you bring them down as far from the body as possible. Exhale on the downward movement. When you reach the lowest point closest to the floor, bend your elbows. Keeping your fingers intertwined, bring your hands up close to your body. Inhale with the upward movement. (Notice that you have made an oval shape with the arms and hands. The continuous movement is like a water wheel.)

Now, in a coordinated movement begin to bend your knees as your arms go down and straighten your knees slightly as your arms go up.

As you find comfort in the practice, begin to engage your entire spine, arching it as you concave the chest. (This movement is like a cat arching its back.) The arms continue to move in an oval direction while the knees continue to bend and straighten. (You might image a luminous egg created by your breathing and movement, connecting the lower and upper parts of your body.) Take a deep breath and relax.

20. Chinese Half Spinal Twist
(Standing recommended) (Chinese Therapeutic Movement)

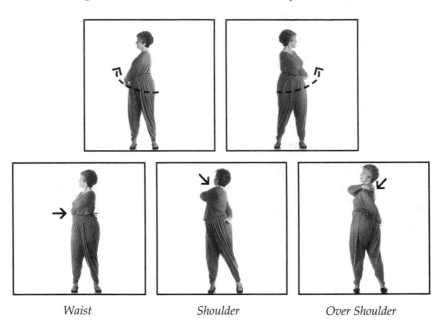

| Waist | Shoulder | Over Shoulder |

Assume original standing position: Feet are shoulder distance apart, knees are slightly bent. Check your posture (long spine, shoulders back, head centered).

With your legs and hips remaining fairly still at first, begin slowly twisting from side to side. Your upper body twists smoothly around to the right, then around to the left. Let your arms swing loosely, and as you start to twist further, begin to bring your legs and hips into motion. Notice how your arms can gently touch your hips as you twist. Now gradually allow your arms to move upward until they gently touch your waist, as you twist, . . . now your shoulders, . . . and over your shoulders, as if you are patting yourself on the back. Now take a deep breath and relax.

21. Yogic Half Spinal Twist
(Sit back down in a chair) (Adaptive Yoga Pose)

 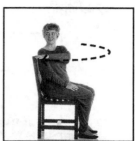

Sit tall in original sitting position as described on page 40.

Extend your left arm forward to shoulder height. Sweep your arm around to the right in the direction of the back of the chair. Move navel, then ribs, and finally the head to the right. Hips are facing forward. Feel the twist in your entire spine. Hold the position while you take 2 or 3 breaths. Focus the mind on the entire spine. Release. Now repeat, extending your right arm, bringing it around to the left of the chair. Be aware of moving in all three areas (navel, ribs, then head.) Hold approximately 2 or 3 breaths. Release. Continue two more times. Shake out any tension. Take a deep breath and relax.

TO BENEFIT LEGS, HIP JOINTS, LOWER BACK

22. Knee to Chest
(Adaptive Yoga Pose)

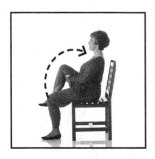

Check your posture as in the previous exercise. Now bend your right knee and bring it up towards your chest. Reach around and clasp the fingers of both of your hands under your knee and gently hug your leg, squeezing it toward your chest. Hold approximately 2 or 3 breaths. Release and relax. Now repeat with the other leg. Bend your left knee and bring it towards your chest. Reach around and grasp under your knee and gently hug your leg, squeezing it toward your chest. Hold approximately 2 or 3 breaths. Release and relax. Continue two more times. Shake out any tension. Take a deep breath. Relax.

23. Leg Extensions
(Adaptive Yoga Pose)

Sit tall in original sitting position as described on page 40.

Extend your right leg forward until parallel to the floor. *Gently press your right heel forward and pull your foot back to stretch your hamstring.* Hold for approximately 3 or 4 breaths. Shake out any tension. Now extend your left leg forward. Press your left heel forward and bring your foot back flexing at the ankle. Hold your left leg approximately 3 or 4 breaths. Shake out any tension. Continue two more times. (You can place your leg on another chair or you can wrap a belt or towel around the foot to help hold the leg up.) Upon completion, take a deep breath.

TO BENEFIT THE KNEES

24. Soup Stirring with the Leg
(Chinese Therapeutic Movement)

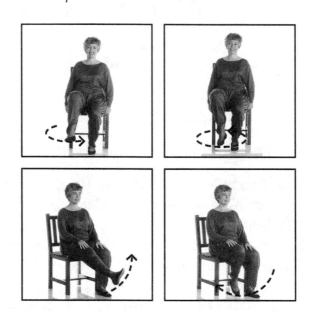

Take original sitting position as described on page 40.

Bend your right knee and lift it slightly, so that your lower leg hangs loose towards the floor. Then begin rotating your lower leg first to the right, then to the left to stir the soup pot. Now move your leg forward and backward to scrape the bottom of the pot. Bring your right leg down and repeat with your other leg. (To perfect balance, this can be done standing. Be sure to have a chair or wall nearby for support.) Continue. Shake out each leg. Take a deep breath and relax. Shake both legs. Take a deep breath and relax.

TO BENEFIT THE ANKLES

25. Soup Stirring with the Foot
(Chinese Therapeutic Movement)

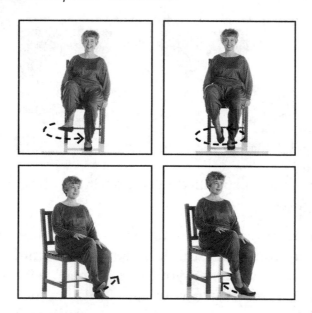

Assume original sitting position as described on page 40.

Lift your right foot off the floor. Rotate your right ankle to the right, then to the left. Now move your ankle back and forth. Repeat. Change sides and begin ankle rotations with your opposite foot. Circle to right, circle to left. Move your ankle back and forth. (For those comfortable balancing on one leg at a time, this, too, can be done standing. Have a chair or wall nearby for support.) Shake both legs. Take a deep breath and relax.

TO BENEFIT THE FEET AND TOES

26. Arching Up
(Preferably with shoes off) (Chinese Therapeutic Movement)

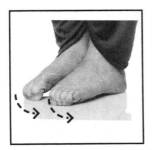 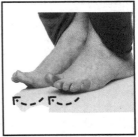

Sit or stand in specified positions. If standing, use chair for support.

Begin to curl your toes under to stretch the arches of your feet. You might think of yourself as making very small feet. Now flex out your toes to make very long and wide feet. Spread open your toes. This practice exercises the arches and stretches the tendons and ligaments in the feet. Continue two more times. Shake out each foot. Take a deep breath and relax.

27. Typewriter Toes
(Preferably with shoes off) (Chinese Therapeutic Movement)

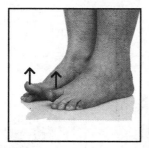
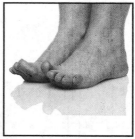

Position One:
Big toe lifted

Position Five:
All five toes lifted

Assume beginning position either standing or sitting. If standing, use chair for support.

Distribute your weight evenly along both feet. Begin to lift your big toes, your second toes, third, fourth and little toes. Notice how the movement is rolling from the inside of the feet to the outside. Now return from your little toes to your big toes, from the outside to the inside of both feet. Continue two more times. Let both feet move from side to side. Shake out each foot. Take a deep breath. Relax.

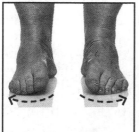
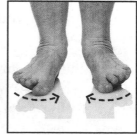

CLOSING
(Adaptive Yoga Pose) (Choose one option)

28. Yogic Seal
(Option One—For Those with Back Difficulties)

Sit tall in a chair with your spine long, shoulders back, head centered. Have your hands in your lap and your feet placed evenly on the floor. This is the beginning position for all of the seated stretches. You may want to place a towel at the area of your lower back for support.

Press your palms in front of your chest with both thumbs touching your breastbone. Lock your thumbs, stretch your arms out in front of you and up over your head with fingertips to the ceiling. Stretch up and hold for a moment, then stretch your arms out as you come down parallel to your thighs. Now place your hands on the upper thighs. Lift your chin and bend forward to the area comfortable for you. (Your chest is towards or on your thighs.) Hold position for 2 or 3 breaths. (If you feel dizzy, lift your chin or come out of the pose at any time.)

To come out of the pose, press your hands against your thighs for support. Keeping your spine stretched out, return your body to an upright position. Bring your palms back in front of your chest. Exhale. Take a deep breath. Relax in the beginning position with your hands back in your lap.

28. Yogic Seal
(Option Two—For Those with Strong Lower Back Muscles)

Sitting in your chair, assume beginning position as described on page 40. Check your posture as in earlier stretches.

Bring your hands behind your back. Grasp your right wrist with your left hand. Close your eyes. Lift your chin and gradually fold forward from the waist. If comfortable, you can lower your head. Keep your awareness within your body. Hold for approximately 2 or 3 breaths. To come out of the pose, lift your chin and slowly raise upward keeping spine stretched outward. Release your hands and place them in your lap. Sit quietly with eyes closed a few minutes and relax.

The yogis say that this pose helps "seal in" the benefits of all the stretches you've done.

NOTICE THE EFFECTS

As you sit still notice how you feel. What is your body temperature? Is there any tingling or other sensations you may not have noticed before the session? Are there any messages your body wants to give you? Be aware of your entire body and how it feels to stretch it into its most natural shape. Experience yourself refreshed and revitalized, and ready for the rest of the day. This is how your body wants to move and deserves to feel each day.

RESTING THE BODY AND USING THE MIND

There may be times when you should not exercise. Situations may occur where you are ill or have injured yourself. At these times the best advice is to rest your body, but review the exercises with your mind. You may be quite surprised to see the results you can receive from doing the stretching practice with your mind alone.

LESSON THREE
Endurance Exercise: A Walking Program

Any activity you enjoy that is continuous, rhythmic and uses large muscles will qualify you for this part of our health program. Examples are: running, swimming, cross-country skiing, biking, rowing, some types of dancing, and good-ole walking.

The *Health and Wholeness* students have adopted a regular walking program. Walking, we believe, provides the most strength and endurance benefits with the lowest risk of injury. And it can be incorporated most easily into daily life, an important factor in sustaining any activity program.

Those with balance or back problems, or who are greatly overweight might consider buying an exercycle and applying the general principles of the walking program to its use. Those with severe arthritis or those unable to walk for other reasons might look into a swimming program. Some communities have special programs for older and/or disabled adults, including wheelchair access into and out of the pool.

But whatever program you choose, be sure you start off slowly. Since many people come into the *Health and Wholeness* class having not exercised regularly for many years, we ease people into the walking gradually. Most begin by walking only five minutes a day, but find by the time the ten-week class is over they have been able to build up to thirty minutes a day with ease.

THE BENEFITS OF MODERATE EXERCISE

Research is now showing that vigorous exercise is not necessary to obtain beneficial results. A landmark study conducted by Dr. Ralph Paffenbarger bears this out. He looked carefully into the relationship between physical activity and longevity of Harvard Alumni over a period of years. He was surprised to find that healthy longevity was more closely related to less strenuous activities such as gardening or walking the dog than to a vigorous aerobic exercise program.

Other research findings by Dr. Steven Blair at the Institute of Aerobics Research and Dr. Arthur Leon at San Francisco's Multiple Risk Factor Intervention Trial (the MR. FIT study) supported Dr. Paffenbarger's work. In both programs, moderate exercise was defined as the equivalent of 30 minutes of walking a day.

SCHEDULING EXERCISE

This is what our heart patients do. They discovered initially that the hardest part of this program was not the thirty minutes of walking itself, but the time they had to set aside to do it.

Most of the heart patients are successful businessmen. And they all lead very active, busy lives. Some of the ways they've carved out time to walk include:

- Walking during lunch hour

- Walking before breakfast or dinner

- Scheduling it in their appointment books each day, along with other important commitments

- Walking every Tuesday and Thursday evenings with the other heart study participants

UNDERSTANDING HEART RATES

Terri Merritt, our exercise physiologist, has worked with each of these heart patients to establish safe exercise limits that achieve desired fitness. First she measures each participant's *resting heart rate*—the number of heart beats per minute while at rest. The goal is to have each participant's heart beat return close to this established resting level as quickly as possible after an exercise session—the quicker it returns to the resting rate, the more fit the person.

Then she helps establish a *maximum heart rate* for each participant. Some of them come to her with the number already identified by their doctors from treadmill testing. For others, she uses the generally accepted formula for estimating maximum heart rate: subtracting their age from the number 220. Terri then identifies the person's *heart rate reserve*, by subtracting their resting heart rate from their maximum heart rate.

She then establishes an individual target heart rate range for each participant. To insure that no one works his or her heart too hard, she sets the upper limit for exercise heart rate at 80% of this number. At the same time, to also insure that the person works his or her heart enough to get some benefit, she sets a lower limit, based on the person's health history, at between 45% and 60% of the heart rate reserve.

Everyone is instructed to work within his or her own target heart rate range. To insure they obtain a training effect (i.e. exercise at their target heart rate), she teaches the patients how to take their pulses while exercising, so they know if they are staying within their designated limits.

For those of you who have difficulty taking your pulse, or dislike working with numbers of any kind, I have good news for you. An important 1986 geriatric study reported in *Medicine and Science in Sports and Exercise* demonstrated that people 67 years and older may not need to count heart beats.

The study showed that older people who worked their hearts at even 35–45% of their heart rate reserve produced cardiovascular changes comparable to those of younger participants in higher-intensity training programs (exercising at 60–70% of heart rate reserves). Since regular-paced walking will normally bring the heart within this lower range and not approach the upper limits, some exercise physiologists suggest that generally healthy older people in such exercise programs do not need to keep pulse rates for their strengthening and endurance programs.

PART TWO

USING THE "INNER TEACHER" INSTEAD

There are other ways to regulate the intensity of exercise, through listening to our bodies. By utilizing our "Inner Teacher," a concept and approach discussed earlier in this book, we can learn signals which tell us clearly the safe range for our exercise. Here are some ways of for making sure you are not exerting your heart too much:

1. *"Whistle While You Work."* Try whistling, singing, or talking as you walk. If you find it difficult, you are working yourself too hard. So slow down until you can talk or make music comfortably.

2. *Give yourself a signal.* You can create your own monitoring scale. Give yourself a signal for what it's like when you're resting, when you're working just right, and when you're tired. Gunnar Borg, a Swedish scientist, developed a standardized Scale for Rate of Perceived Exertion (RPE), with numbers from 6 to 20. Six was equivalent to lying down and doing nothing. Twenty was the hardest work you'd ever done. His recommended range was between 11 and 15.

You can modify this scale to meet your needs. Those of you with a musical ear can learn to identify a range of body sounds: soprano sounds for working too hard; bass sounds for too low; alto to tenor for just right. The body does this naturally. Listen for its natural squeaks, its groans, its hums.

Or you could choose colors or images. Anything will do. The important point is to listen to your body. Gunnar Borg demonstrated through his now accepted scale that we all

77

have the capacity to perceive, and therefore to measure our own level of exertion without counting heart beats.

THE HEALTH AND WHOLENESS WALKING PRESCRIPTION

Here is the walking prescription for our program:

Week	Warm-Up Stretches	Continuous Walking	Cool-Down Stretches
1st	5–10 minutes	5 minutes	5–10 minutes
2nd	5–10 minutes	7 minutes	5–10 minutes
3rd	5–10 minutes	10 minutes	5–10 minutes
4th	5–10 minutes	12 minutes	5–10 minutes
5th	5–10 minutes	15 minutes	5–10 minutes
6th	5–10 minutes	18 minutes	5–10 minutes
7th	5–10 minutes	20 minutes	5–10 minutes
8th	5–10 minutes	25 minutes	5–10 minutes
9th	5–10 minutes	27 minutes	5–10 minutes
10th	5–10 minutes	30 minutes	5–10 minutes

But before you begin, let's work with awareness.

EXERCISE 3–1
A WALKING AWARENESS EXERCISE

Slowly stand up. Take a deep breath. You may begin to notice how your body weight is distributed along your feet. Are you more aware of the toes of the feet or the heels? Which foot holds most of the weight, right or left? Which side of the foot? Feel your weight evenly balanced and the ground completely supporting your feet.

Become aware of your arms. Your hands.

How tall do you feel? Imagine a golden cord lifting you upward without strain until you are the height you are supposed to be. Notice your posture. Experience your chest opening. Become aware of your entire spine from your lower back to your middle back. Notice how your neck is long and lifted. Your internal organs have all the space they need.

What is it like to stand in perfect posture—spine erect, shoulders back, head centered, weight balanced right to left and top to bottom?

Step slowly forward on your right heel and focus attention on how it touches the floor. Feel the weight being shifted along the right foot and then forward to the toes. Notice that the left heel is lifting, the instep is lifting, as the weight is being shifted forward to the toes. Move each foot so slowly that you can experience the bones, the joints, the ligaments as they become engaged in this motion. Continue.

On the next step become aware of your hips. Then your trunk . . . Then arms. Notice how the simple task of walking involves the whole body, head to toes.

As you walk, you may want to focus on your breath. Choose a breathing rhythm. You might inhale as you place weight on the right leg, and exhale on the left. Or you might find another more comfortable rhythm for your body.

Just keep your mind focused on your body and your breath. Notice how you can maintain an outward awareness of your environment (where you are placing you foot, where you are going), while at the same time maintaining an inward one (noting each movement of your body and how it feels).

BEGIN WITH SAFETY

1. Discuss this walking program with your doctor. This is especially important for those of you who have not been in a regular exercise program for some time, who have had your activity restricted for any reason in the past, and those at least fifty percent overweight. Other conditions that require a medical clearance are lung problems, diabetes, heart problems, high blood pressure, and any regimen of heart medications.

2. Wear safe, comfortable shoes. Be sure you have shoes with arch-support and good traction, and that are shock-absorbing.

3. Dress in layers. Remember, your body will heat up as you walk. This way you can add or shed clothing for comfort. In cold weather, you may find that a woolen hat and mittens help you retain body heat.

4. Always listen to your body and adjust your pace to what is right for you.

5. Remember to "Warm-Up" and "Cool-Down " before and after each exercise session.

6. Practice deep three-part breathing before and after exercising.

"WARM-UPS"

After some deep three-part breathing, there will be five to ten minutes of "Warm-Ups" before each walk. You can use either the *Walking Awareness Exercise* or some stretches from the first part of this chapter to prepare your body for endurance exercise—or a combination of both. But if you use the stretches, be sure to include those focusing on the lower body, especially the legs and feet. Stretches 22 through 27 would be good ones.

CONTINUOUS EXERCISE

Begin to walk at your natural pace. As you walk, keep your external awareness high. Be aware of your environment, the cracks in the sidewalk, any curbs, any on-coming traffic. But also maintain your inner awareness, always listening to your body.

Keep track of your level of exertion, using one of the methods that enlist the "Inner Teacher" to make sure you aren't trying to do too much. And notice, appreciate, and enjoy the intricacies of how your body walks.

To work your upper body, curl your fingers slightly, and be sure to move them as briskly as you move your legs. Some people who want to increase upper body exercise and increase their heart rate carry weights in their hands or strap them to their wrists or arms, allowing them to pump back and forth with their walking stride.

Find a comfortable pace, one you can maintain in a rhythmic, continuous fashion for the number of minutes prescribed. It's better to keep a slow, even pace than make a lot of quick starts and stops. Just like the tortoise and the hare, it's the tortoise-style that tends to win when your goal is optimum health.

"COOL-DOWNS"

After you have kept a steady pace for the prescribed time, start your "Cool-Down" by gradually slowing down for five to ten minutes, returning to your "Walking Awareness" speed. You can also do some more stretches.

BE SURE TO "WARM-UP," "COOL-DOWN," AND BREATHE

Some people want to skimp on the "Warm-Up" and "Cool-Down" sections. Don't. They are very important, to avoid injuries and muscle soreness, as well as cardiovascular problems. Also, if you do not "Cool-Down," blood can pool in your legs and you can feel dizzy or lightheaded, and get muscle cramps.

Finally, to insure oxygen reserve, end with some deep three-part breathing.

THE MENTAL APPROACH

After the first class most people can experience the physical benefits of both the stretching and dynamic movements. However, I am happy to tell you that the best is yet to come.

By focusing your mind on the areas of the body being benefited, you increase the effectiveness of each movement. Putting it simply, the body and mind are both more powerful when they work together. More blood can be directed to specific locations. Muscles in strategic spots can become strengthened or relaxed, when the mind sends a clear direction.

Physical benefits can be obtained to some degree when doing several things at once. But to get the full benefit of the body/mind connection, you must focus on the practice alone. That is why you should not do the stretches while participating in any other activity, such as watching T.V., riding in a car, or worrying about your taxes. We also recommend that when walking, your mind should stay focused, inward on the body and outward only to the level required for safety or to experience the other body/mind/spirit aspects of the walking program.

With a focused mind, you can both avoid injury and enjoy maximum physical benefits. But there are more payoffs. Learning to focus your mind on one thing at a time is not an easy task, especially in our culture. When we do, however, we increase our ability to concentrate, an invaluable skill in our busy fragmented society. Among other things, the ability to concentrate is vital for learning, as well as for the storage of that learning which directly affects our memory.

When we get to the meditation and visualization chapter, we'll also discover how a focused mind can reduce tension, allow us to feel more alert, and assist in the healing of our bodies.

EMOTIONAL BENEFITS

Moving our bodies definitely gives us a better mental outlook. We can not only build strength, but also confidence, self-esteem, and our general sense of well-being. We can feel good about how we look and what we have accomplished.

But there is evidence of even further emotional benefits. Exercising can release endorphins, chemicals in our brain that produce this sense of well-being. Some patients have been given guidelines to help them match their exercise programs to their specific psychological needs. For example, those suffering from depression might be instructed to take brisk walks daily with friends. On the other hand, those dealing with anxiety might be told to take quiet walks along scenic paths.

Dr. Robert Hale, psychiatrist and co-author of *The U.S. Army Total Fitness Program*, recommends a walking program to go along with his psychotherapy treatment. He even specifies when his patients should exercise. For alcoholics, for example, he suggests morning walks done in groups. For Type-A heart patients he prescribes solo walks in the early evening.

THE SPIRITUAL APPROACH

If a movement program is so beneficial, and makes us feel so good, why then, is it such a struggle for us to do it each day? Quite simply, healthy habits require discipline, and for most of us training of any sort is simply unappealing. In fact, most of us would prefer to live in pain and discomfort, rather than discipline ourselves to do something healthy. Dr. Dean Ornish, the director of the Preventive Medicine Research Institute says, "We'll choose our personal freedom over our health any day."

So how can we remain free and also exercise? *Health and Wholeness* students have learned two ways to make it easier. One, is to exercise together when at all possible—in a class, or at home with a friend or spouse.

This can be very helpful when it's practical, but most of us can't go to a class every day of the week, or find a spouse or friend even occasionally who is willing to follow our routine at a time suitable for us both. *Health and Wholeness* students found, therefore, that over the long haul, a second way was more beneficial. They learned to do the practices along with a type of daily worship.

Now this might sound strange. But yoga came about, not so much to improve the physical health of monks, but to improve their physical ability to sit longer in prayer. For them, the yogic stretches and breathing practices always preceded their daily meditations.

Most of my students have some form of daily routine—reading the *Bible*, repeating a prayer, having a special thought for the day. They have found that if the health practices are done in concert with a daily spiritual ritual they have already established, the health promotion practices are no longer chores to dread but pleasures to anticipate. Two experiences will help illustrate the point:

> *Before I do my stretching, I put on some lovely meditation music. When I begin the Sun Salutation, I always say a prayer. It's amazing the difference it's made.*

Another student says this:

> *I've never been the churchgoing-type. Don't say prayers and don't intend to start. But since this class, I do take some deep breaths and think of a special beach where I like to go. This way I connect stretching with my times at the beach. I don't know, if you'd call that spiritual and all. But it works for me.*

WITH ENDURANCE EXERCISE

The endurance exercise portion can be done with the same spirit. The student mentioned earlier can actually walk on his beach. You can choose your own place of beauty.

Open your heart and your senses as you walk. You can begin by noticing the change of seasons. Before you know it, you'll have made good friends with the trees and foliage along your way. And after a while they may even begin to communicate with you.

Or you can walk as a way of giving service to others. I have a friend who picks up trash in his neighborhood as he walks. One *Health and Wholeness* student walks the dog of a disabled friend. Perhaps there's a small child in the neighborhood who could use some daily attention.

In certain African traditions, members of the tribe were honored and supported through sustained dance and movement. If a warrior died, the women joined his widow in her hut and grieved together. The men banded together in symbolic dance and ritualistic movement that might last for hours, even days. This exercise was, I believe, of a spiritual nature—one done in honor of and with respect for another.

We can create our own traditions. Each time we walk we can dedicate the walk to someone we love. Think of someone who can't walk—who is ill, home-bound, troubled, perhaps has died. By honoring this person (even yourself), you give meaning to your practice.

And it is meaning that makes life worth living. Purposeful exercise raises the spirit and makes the task worthy of your time.

SPIRITUAL HEALTH: THE KEY TO DISCIPLINE

What exactly is spiritual health? *Health and Wholeness* students define this concept broadly—anything that brings you closer to yourself, to other people, or to a higher source. When you begin the various activities in this book, think of how you can serve or respect yourself and others through your efforts. When you can do this, you will have found your own key that will unlock the secret for sustaining a body/mind/spirit practice.

PART TWO

RECOMMENDED EXERCISE PROGRAM FOR HEALTH

FOR OPTIMAL HEALTH

1. Do the entire set of stretches each day with a body/mind/spirit focus.

2. Begin an endurance exercise program appropriate to your level of conditioning, working towards 30 minutes of continuous walking (or other physical activity) per day.

TO FEEL BETTER

1. Pick those stretches that relieve the tension or pain in a certain part of the body.

2. Pick different stretches for each day.

3. Begin walking up the stairs, instead of taking elevators.

4. Park as far from your destination as feasible. Better yet, walk instead of driving whenever you can.

5. Do some sustained, endurance exercise—once a week, three times a week, whatever amount will work for you. A little exercise is better than none at all.

PRECAUTIONS

Any time you feel any pain, stress, dizziness or unsteadiness of any kind, stop and rest. You can always try it again

89

at another time or another day. And when you can't do the physical exercise, you can still get some benefit from doing the stretching practice using only your mind.

Do not jerk your body or hold your breath while stretching. Breathe normally, with some deep breathing between each stretch.

When doing the standing stretches, be sure to have a chair or wall nearby for support. Always be sure your standing surface is slip-proof.

Obtain your doctor's permission before beginning a endurance exercise program. When walking, wear safe, comfortable shoes, with arch-support and non-slip soles. Always do some level of "Warm-Up" or "Cool-Down" and some deep three-part breathing.

See a doctor, if you experience any of these symptoms when exercising: chest pain, shortness of breath, irregular heart beats, dizziness, extreme fatigue.

PERSONAL STRETCHING GOAL

I will practice the following therapeutic stretches (list by name or number)

daily for approximately _____ weeks and notice how I feel.

I will begin the following endurance exercise program for _____ weeks and notice how I feel.

	Warm-Ups (no. of mins.)	Continuous (no. of mins.)	Cool-Down (no. of mins.)
1st			
2nd			
3rd			
4th			
5th			
6th			
7th			
8th			
9th			
10th			

I will focus my mind by:

I will combine my exercises with what to me is spiritual by:

P R O G R E S S   R E P O R T

Date

_____

What Done

_____

_____

_____

_____

Improvements Noticed

_____

_____

_____

_____

_____

_____

Reported to Whom

_____

FURTHER READING

ENDURANCE EXERCISE

BLAIR, S.M., H. S. Kohl, and R. S. Paffenbarger. "Physical Fitness and All-Cause Mortality." *Journal of the American Medical Association*, (1989) 262:2395-24–1.

BORG, G.V. "The Borg Scale for Rate of Perceived Exertion." *Medical Science Sports Exercise.* (1982), 14:377–87.

DE VRIES, H. A., and G. M. Adams. *Fitness After 50: An Exercise Prescription for Lifelong Health.* New York: Charles Scribners' Sons, 1982.

HALES, Dianne and Robert Hales. "Using the Body to Mend the Mind." *American Health.* (June 1985), 27–31.

KEMPER, Donald W., E. Judith Deneen, and James V. Giuffre. *Growing Younger Handbook.* Boise, ID: A Healthwise Publication, 3rd ed., 1987.

Medical Science Sports Exercise. (1983), 15:496–502.

ORNISH, Dean. *Dr. Dean Ornish's Program for Reversing Heart Disease.* New York: Ballantine Books, 1992.

PAFFENBARGER, R. S., R. T. Jude, and A. L. Wing. "Physical Activity, All-Cause Mortality, and Longevity of College Alumni." *New England Journal of Medicine.* (1986), 314:605–13.

SMITH, E.L., and R.C. Serfass. *Exercise and Aging: The Scientific Basis.* Hillside, N. J.: Enslow Publishers, 1981.

YOGIC STRETCHES

BELL, Lorna and Eudor Seyfer. *Gentle Yoga for People with Arthritis, Stroke Damage, Multiple Sclerosis and in Wheelchairs.* Cedar Rapids, Iowa: Ingram Press, 3rd ed., 1984.

CHRISTENSEN, Alice and David Rankin. *Easy Does It Yoga for Older People.* New York: Harper and Row, 2nd ed., 1979.

FOLAN, Lilias. "Nice and Easy Yoga." *Lilias, Yoga and Your Life.* New York: Collier Book, 1981.

FOLAN, Lilias. *Forever Flexible: The Easy Stretching Program for a More Vital You.* Rudra Press, P.O. 1973–L, Cambridge, MA 02238, 1-(800)-876-7798 (Video Tape for older adults).

NISCHALANANDA, Swami. *Extra Gentle Integral Yoga Hatha: Designed for Senior Citizens, the Physically Challenged, or People Who Have Been Physically Inactive.* Yogaville, VA: Satchidananda Ashram, 1986. (Audio Tape)

SATCHIDANANDA, Sri Swami. *Integral Yoga Hatha.* New York: Holt, Rinehart and Winston, 1970.

SCHELLER, Mary Dale. *Staying Well Through: The Body, Mind and Spirit.* San Francisco Community College District, Older Adult Program, 106 Bartlett, San Francisco, CA, 94110 (Document)

CHINESE STRETCHES

CHANG, Stephen T. with Richard C. Miller. *The Book of Internal Exercises.* San Francisco: Strawberry Hill Press, 1978.

GACH, Michael Reed. *Eight Essential Standing Exercises. Introduction to Acupressure.* The Acupressure Institute, 1533 Shattuck, Berkely, CA, 94709.

SCHELLER, Mary Dale with Neil Douglas-Klotz. *Chinese Therapeutic Movements.* Dances of Universal Peace, P.O. Box 626, Fairfax, CA, 94930. (Document)

POINT THREE

Dining with the "Inner Teacher":
A New Approach to Eating Well and Drinking Water

He who would attain enlightenment
must first conquer the palate.
ANCIENT EASTERN SAYING

You are what you eat.
CONTEMPORARY WESTERN SAYING

We need to get the following essential nutrients from our food:

Protein

—mainly to build and repair body tissues.

Carbohydrates and Fats

—mainly to supply fuel and energy for our bodies to function.

Minerals (calcium, phosphorus, iron and copper, iodine, sodium, potassium, chlorine, trace elements)

—mainly to build and maintain bone structure and teeth and the regulate bodily processes.

Vitamins (A, B-complex, C, D, E, K, folacin)

—mainly to promote growth and maintain health.

Water

—mainly to promote digestion, absorption, circulation and excretion as well as to maintain body temperature, hydration and lubrication.

LESSON FOUR
Eating Well

When I began to teach nutrition in my health promotion classes, I often became frustrated. On one hand, I was amazed at the nutritional knowledge we had acquired as a culture, yet puzzled by the difficulty of using that knowledge effectively.

All my students knew the essential nutrients, the basic food groups, the recommended dietary allowances—in essence, my nutrition course. They left me little to teach.

Most could discourse on the physiology of aging. They knew that their metabolism had slowed down, that they needed to eat less food and exercise more or they would gain weight. They already understood how health problems associated with aging (such as dental problems and poor bowel function) affected what they ate.

Many talked about how living alone influenced what foods they were willing to cook and eat. They understood only too well how the physical and psychosocial aspects of aging had affected their food choices and eating habits. And they all knew the requirements for a healthful and wholesome diet.

ELEMENTS OF A WHOLESOME DIET

A wholesome diet, they could tell me, was one that was:

- high in complex carbohydrates
- high in fiber

- low in fat

- low in salt

- low in sugar

- unprocessed

They also knew that with regard to food choices, emphasis should be on fresh vegetables, fresh fruits, and whole grains.

Regardless of their educational or income levels, my students understood a great deal about nutritional theory. Mainly from their doctors and from health topics presented by the media, they had acquired an adequate nutritional knowledge base. Yet, for some reason that I couldn't fully understand, very few were able to put their knowledge into practice.

And this irony, I believe, is true for not only the older population where I teach, but for all ages of American culture. It is certainly true of my family and me.

Here we are an agriculturally-rich country that offers access to whatever food we want in whatever season. We don't have to wait in line for milk. We can have bananas, tomatoes, strawberries almost year round. We can purchase oranges from Florida, salmon from Alaska, mangoes from Hawaii—all in the same supermarket. And many stores are open 7-days-a-week, some 24-hours-a-day.

And although there are hungry people in this country, as a nation we try not to limit our food supply to only those who can pay for it. Food stamps, nutrition programs for the elderly, and school lunch programs for our children all insure that some level of access to wholesome foods is available at reasonable prices or at no cost to most population groups.

PERSONALLY RELATING TO HEALTHY EATING

So I began to realize that the missing link I was looking for was not the lack of nutritional information nor the availability of good, wholesome food, but the inability of most of us to personally relate to healthy eating. Our educational programs focused on *the quality of the food*. Our national policy focused on *the accessibility of the food*.

What I now hoped to offer was some discourse on *the social and emotional aspects of eating this food*. And through our awareness, hopefully to provide the right atmosphere, where we could better utilize our knowledge, and integrate more healthy eating habits into our total living experience.

EXERCISE 4–1
A CLASS EXERCISE FOR EATING AWARENESS

Pick a small portion of some healthy food—a slice of carrot, 2 or 4 grapes, a wedge of orange, a rice cracker, whatever. Before you place it in your mouth, notice the color, the size, its texture, fibers, the temperature in your hand.

Now smell this piece of food. Are there any memories or feelings associated with this aroma? What are they? How long ago? Did it involve another person? Was the experience pleasant? Unpleasant? Try to bring the memory clearly into your consciousness.

When you are ready, place this piece of food in your mouth. But before you begin to chew, feel it with your tongue. Let it touch your teeth, your gums, the insides of your cheeks. Notice now with your mouth the texture, size, fibers, temperature. Enjoy the full sensation. If you are aware of any memories or associations, let them surface and fully experience them.

Now slowly begin to chew with your mind completely focused on each bite. Savor the taste, notice if it changes as you chew. Notice what teeth you use to chew.

Are you chewing more on the right or on the left side of your mouth? Observe the action of your jaw, your tongue. Enjoy the juice you are creating, before you slowly begin to swallow each bite. Finally, if you wish to do so, give thanks in your own way for this nourishment you are now receiving.

Some of my students called this exercise a "biofoodback experiment." And that response gave me a handle to begin to grasp and define what we had undertaken to do.

Biofeedback is a method that lets the mind know numerically exactly how the body is reacting to a given stimulus (e.g., a technique like deep breathing, deep relaxation, visualization). Perhaps as a class, I hoped we could begin to involve our minds, and eventually our spirits, in the service of good nutrition.

First, it seemed important that we develop a better communication link between our bodies and our minds regarding our nutritional needs and experiences. And then, together we could try to make more conscious choices—buy healthier foods, eat more realistic amounts, and experience more pleasurable dining situations, based on our bodies' true physiological needs and not just on our minds' emotional ones.

But first we had to identify and separate the needs of our bodies from the needs of our minds. Only then could we hope to satisfy both body and mind in healthy rather than unhealthy ways.

"The Inner Teacher"

I've often wondered why so many of those who begin a serious yoga practice are able within a short time, without education or prompting, to change their diets. The same is often true I've noticed with those who've involved themselves in some type of comprehensive self-help program. When people begin to truly tune in to themselves, they become aware of what they really need. When they begin consciously to improve one part of their lives, other parts improve as well.

Thus yoga, for example, becomes more than a program to help bodies become more flexible; Alcoholics Anonymous becomes more than a program to help people stay sober. Through such programs participants have become more sensitive and aware. And at some level, whether these people use our name for it or not, I believe they've enlisted the help of the "Inner Teacher."

Awareness is the Key

You may be surprised to know that the breathing and stretching practices, along with other aspects of the *Health and Wholeness* program, actually help us develop a well-balanced nutritional life. You see, these practices take us inward.

Only when we quiet ourselves down, can we really hear our innermost needs. We must listen to our feelings, our desires, our emotional conflicts, and identify our deepest psychological pain as well as our physical pain and hunger. Only when we are able to distinguish between them will we begin to satisfy psychic needs through emotional means, and nutritional needs through food.

Awareness is the key. When we are sensitive to ourselves, we can be more aware of our choices. When we make wrong choices, we can learn from them.

Instead of just suffering with an allergic reaction for example, we can find out what our nutritional needs are, in the same way that scientists do.

You might find yourself saying, "That's interesting. I put milk and sugar on my cereal this morning, and look what's happening: my nose is stuffy; there is mucous in my throat; I feel jumpy and irritable. Maybe I should go without dairy products and sugar for a few days and see if it makes a difference."

That's exactly what allergists do. They have you note the effects of specific foods on your body. We can all benefit from this sort of conscious food inquiry.

Good nutrition, I believe, requires an openness to self-study and self-awareness. This is because we can really only sustain an improved diet when we are ready to improve our whole being—body, mind, and spirit. That was the ancient way of the East.

THE ANCIENT WAY OF THE EAST

Both Indian and Chinese nutritional teachings seek to broaden the consciousness of the student. In fact, many traditional Chinese physicians would not treat patients unless they were willing to examine and to change their diets as part of the treatment. Dr. Mary Austin in her classic book, *The Textbook of Acupuncture Therapy*, writes, "Among the most important of all external circumstances and habits that militate against complete [acupuncture] cure is diet . . . Do not expect your patient to be cured so long as faulty diet persists."

Both the Indian and the Chinese systems look seriously at not only the physical value of food for the body, but what it does for the mental state as well. They also look at how emotional attitude affects the selection of the food we eat, as well as its digestion and assimilation. In Eastern practice, the body, mind and spirit always go together.

104

PART TWO

Look for Similarities

Let's look at some basic concepts from the Indian and Chinese disciplines. When I look at different nutritional systems, I can easily get confused. So what I do and what I recommend that you do as we compare these two Eastern systems with our Western tradition, is not to focus on the contradictions, but instead, look for the similarities. I believe that whenever such different cultures, functioning with uniquely different theories and philosophies, different agricultural conditions, and different traditions and customs, can agree on anything, there is a suggestion of some kind of universal truth.

THE YOGIC (INDIAN) APPROACH TO NUTRITION

Yoga philosophy concerns itself with three basic properties. In this case, we are talking about three states of the mind:

Sattva is tranquil, balanced, cheerful, with mental clarity.

Rajas is active, restless, confused, frenetic.

Tamas is dull, irritable, lazy, lethargic.

With the yogic approach, you can choose the emotional state you want by choosing the food you eat.

Sattvic Foods	Rajasic Foods	Tamasic Foods
whole grains	meat	overripe, stale, burnt, rot-
fresh ripe fruits	fish	ten, fermented foods
fresh vegetables	eggs	(e.g.,leftovers, charcoaled
honey	onions	foods, cheese, alcohol)
nuts	garlic	foods with additives (e.g.,
	spices in	preservatives, artificial
	excess	coloring, emulsifiers)

105

The yogic practitioner would approach dietary choices in the same way as a Western nutritionist—that is, in terms of your goals. In other words, if you want to lower your cholesterol in our culture, your doctor or nutritionist would advise you regarding the food you should eat and the foods you should avoid.

The yogic practitioner would apply his advice to the mental state you desired as well. If you wanted to be tranquil while retaining mental clarity, you should eat sattvic foods. If you need a little energy, you might add a little onion or garlic to your food, but not enough to create confusion or restlessness.

They would look also at *how* you eat. You could choose a healthy sattvic diet, but if you ate in a frenetic, rajastic manner, it could make you restless and rajastic. On the other hand, if you had a sattvic meal, but overate, you could become sleepy and dull, experiencing a tamasic condition.

In focusing on the how of eating, the yogic approach to food is not concerned just about *what* you eat, but how eating affects all aspects of your life. For instance, which foods give you the greatest "inner peace"? Which ones lead to your highest conscious state?

For the serious student of yoga, the diet is believed to take on spiritual significance. Controlling the senses (called pratyahara) is an important part of the yogic spiritual practice. Their sages teach that the tongue's sense of taste and associated appetite is the most powerful of the senses and the most difficult to control. Only when one has controlled this drive can spiritual development proceed.

CHINESE MEDICINE APPROACH TO NUTRITION

Chinese philosophy works a little differently. It believes that the life force is organized around the combination of two energies. *Yang* is male energy—active, contractive. *Yin* is female energy—receptive, expansive.

Health, in Chinese tradition, requires a balance of these opposing forces. Therefore, a Chinese physician would assess your basic condition (your body appearance, your personality, the health conditions you present) before recommending a diet. If you were too *yin,* he or she might recommend a *yang* diet. If you were too *yang*, you should eat more *yin* foods.

According to this theory no food is bad or good in itself, nor does the method of preparation affect its wholesomeness. It is a matter of the kind required for a given person to achieve balance. The goal of nutrition, like all other aspects of Chinese medicine, is to get the energy of your body into balance.

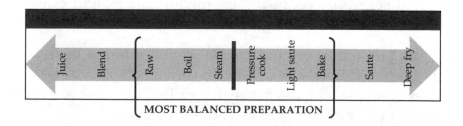

All food, as well as the means of food preparation, is allocated a place on a Yin-Yang continuum. The most balanced foods are placed in parenthesis.

THE AREA OF AGREEMENT

Now here's what's important—what both the Indian and Chinese cultures agree on for a healthful, balanced diet: fresh vegetables, whole grains, and fresh fruits in moderation. And this is what nutrition educators in the United States are increasingly emphasizing in the American diet.

A Cross-Cultural Study

Taking this still further, there is a definite correlation between these diet recommendations and research evidence on healthy longevity.

Dr. Alexander Leaf, a distinguished American physician on the Harvard Medical School faculty, went to remote corners of the world to study the lifestyle of three societies where elders in the community lived to be very old. These areas—the district of Abkhazia in the Caucasus Mountains (of the former USSR), the province of Hunza in the Karakoram Mountains of northwestern Pakistan, and the isolated village of Vilcabamba in the Andes Mountains of Ecuador—have attracted international interest, both general and scientific, because their inhabitants exhibit more than just longevity.

You see, these very old people were not found bedridden in their homes or in wheelchairs at nursing homes. They were plowing the fields and leading the same active, useful lives they had lived as younger people.

108

Comparing the three environments, Dr. Leaf found several similarities: all lived at high altitudes in rural areas; there was a remarkably high level of physical fitness and activity; obesity was practically nonexistent; and their diets were low in calories and in animal fats.

Dr. Kenneth Pelletier, Professor at the University of California Medical School in San Francisco and author of *Longevity: Fulfilling our Biological Potential*, examines in his book the possible factors leading to this long life: genetics, nutrition, physical activity, sexual activity, social environment, and physical environment. He concludes, "After genetic endowment, the second common denominator conducive to longevity found in observations of centenarians is nutritional and dietary practice."

The Vilcabambas ate from their land, living on a diet almost exclusively of vegetables and grains. Similarly, the diet of the Hunzakuts relied primarily on grains, leafy green vegetables, root vegetables, dried legumes, fresh milk and buttermilk, clarified butter and cheese, fresh and sun-dried apricots, mulberries, and grape wine. The Abkhazian, although also consuming some animal products from the dairy component of their economy, relied on diets that still were considerably higher in fiber and complex carbohydrate, and lower in salt and sugar than our typical American fare.

SCIENTIFIC-BASED ADVICE FOR AMERICANS

The Ornish diet that led to reversal of heart disease was similar to the above diets in that it consisted of fresh fruits, vegetables, grains, legumes and soybean products. However, it differed in that it eliminated caffeine and all oils and animal products, including fish and chicken. Dr. Ornish states. "Half-way measures such as eating less red meat, eating more fish and chicken with the skin removed—aren't enough to reverse coronary heart disease for the majority of people . . . Only a diet almost entirely free of animal fat, oil, and cholesterol will significantly lower blood cholesterol levels reliably and lead to reversal of coronary artery disease."

Although other scientists are less stringent in their dietary recommendations, they do tend to prescribe along similar lines. Drs. James F. Fries and Lawrence M. Crapo, both professors at Stanford Medical School, follow current research that correlates diet and exercise with healthy aging. In their book, *Vitality and Aging,* they state that it is our unhealthy eating habits and unnatural lifestyles, not the aging process per se that is leading us to chronic disease in old age and premature death.

What type of diet do they recommend for healthy aging? "We counsel . . . and believe, until (contrary) evidence is in, that a moderately low salt, low animal fat, high-fiber, low refined carbohydrate diet is indicated for most people."

EXERCISE 4–2
SIMPLE NUTRITION TIPS

Here are some simple nutrition tips our *Health and Wholeness* students have put together for their own use:

GROCERY SHOPPING

1. Make a U-Turn around the outer aisles at the grocery store! If you shop only on the outside aisles of most grocery stores, you'll only have access to fruits, vegetables, dairy products, and the like. Our freshest food requires refrigeration, and refrigeration requires electrical outlets, usually placed on the outside walls. Just notice. Cookies, potato chips, crackers, and other processed foods in most supermarkets are in the middle aisles.

2. Shop only with a full stomach and with a grocery list.

3. Purchase food in its original natural state. (If you had to shell every peanut, walnut, or pecan you ate, chances are you wouldn't eat as many as you would if they had been shelled, salted, and were waiting for you in a can.)

FOOD PREPARATION

1. Eat the food in its original natural state. You'll get more fiber, retain more nutrients, and usually eat fewer calories. Just think about it: one fresh apple will satisfy most appetites; on the other hand, a 6-ounce

111

glass of apple juice or a moderate serving of apple sauce might contain the equivalent of 3 to 5 apples—and you're still left hungry.

2. Cook food for as short a time as possible. Cooking can deplete mineral and vitamin content. When cooking, a quick steaming is often best.

3. Saute with water or fruit juices. Much of the time you do not have to use any additional oils or other fats in food preparation.

DINING WITH THE "INNER TEACHER"

1. Quiet yourself before you eat. If so inclined, say a blessing or a prayer. If you don't have one that feels right to you, take three deep breaths. Our students found they ate less and digested their food better when they began their meals in this way.

2. Stay aware. Notice what you are about to eat. Plan your amounts ahead of time. Chew and swallow with awareness and full enjoyment. If you are unable to do this, you may need to practice the "Eating Awareness Exercise" outlined earlier in this chapter.

3. Stay calm and focused during meal times. Some people have found they have to eat alone, especially if their eating companions complain or create discord during dinner. Others who normally eat alone have found they need to eliminate outside distractions. Often this means turning off T.V. or putting down the newspaper until after the meal is over.

4. Keep a *"Diet Awareness Chart,"* where you list the date, time, location, and mood you are in as you are eating. Many people find this helps them have more control over their eating habits; and it heightens their awareness levels as well.

5. Don't eat if angry or after receiving bad news. Your emotions affect how you digest your food.

6. Keep a "light" mind to have a "light" body. Most people eat more when anxious, fearful or worried. If you worry all the time about overeating, guess what you'll most likely do? Overeat! As you think, so you will become. So as a yoga teacher of mine advises, "If the body is on the heavy side, keep the mind light."

An upcoming chapter on positive imagery discusses how we actually become the image we create for ourselves. Practice seeing yourself as healthy and at the weight that's right for you.

7. I approach nutrition with a body/mind/spirit perspective. Remember it's important what you eat. But equally important are who you eat it with, and the attitude you have as you eat.

At a body/mind/spirit level, everything is important. I could cook for you the most nutritious meal possible, full of fresh produce, including all the food elements in the right amounts for your particular body size, and prepared lovingly in the healthiest of ways. I could set the table with my best china, light some candles and place before you a dozen red roses. The atmosphere could be ever so delightful, the food full of nourishment. But if you were angry at me or the person sitting across from you, or if you were sad and depressed for any reason, you could not optimally digest the food and assimilate the nutrients, despite all of my efforts.

LESSON FIVE
Drinking Water

Our bodies are approximately 70% water. And we lose water constantly through urination, perspiration, and respiration. To remain healthy and to sustain life, we must daily replenish our water supplies.

"If it is possible to say that one essential nutrient is more essential than another," writes Dr. Helen Guthrie in her classic text, *Introductory Nutrition*, "we would have to concede that it is water." We can live for weeks or even years without certain essential vitamins and minerals, she explains. But without water, we could survive for only a few days.

WHAT WATER DOES FOR THE BODY

1. Eliminates toxins from the body through adequate urination

2. Helps kidneys function properly

3. Aids in digestion

4. Helps prevent constipation

5. Aids in circulation by increasing blood volume

6. Helps maintain muscle tone

7. Prevents drying of connective tissue, ligaments, tendons, nerves, organs, cells

8. Serves as a lubricant around joints

9. Serves as a shock absorber inside the eyes, spinal cord, amniotic sac in pregnancy

10. Maintains cellular health, assists in cell growth and division

11. Regulates body temperature, prevents heat exhaustion and heat stroke

12. Helps prevent mental fatigue and memory problems

For those trying to lose weight:

1. Helps satisfy appetite

2. Helps the body metabolism (utilize) food

RECOMMENDED WATER ALLOWANCE FOR MOST PEOPLE

We can lose over $2^1/2$ quarts of water a day through urine, feces, perspiration, and expiration. But we can replenish this amount through the liquids we drink, and the foods we eat, and to a limited extent through our production of water as we metabolize food.

To insure that we maintain an adequate water balance, many health educators recommend that their students drink at least two quarts of water a day. To make sure they get their allotment, many people prepare a quart pitcher and empty it twice each day; or simply keep track and make sure they drink 8 eight-ounce glasses.

The Individual Approach Through Response to Thirst

With the body/mind/spirit approach, we seek to find a way that the body can speak to the mind about one's individual needs. There can be many ways to do this, better ways than relying on the body sensation we most often use—our thirst.

Unfortunately, thirst is a poor indicator of the water needs of the body. Often a person has to be seriously dehydrated before the thirst mechanism goes into action. It's somewhat like the red warning light on the dashboard of our car—if we wait for the red light to blink before we put oil in our car, we can be in trouble. For optimal health we need to find a method that sends a water signal earlier than thirst.

Relying on Color Instead

Dr. Jim Wilkerson, an instructor for the Mountain Medicine Institute (which offers classes for physicians through the University of California School of Medicine at San Francisco), recommends that we learn to monitor the color of our urine. If we have met the water needs of our body, he states, our urine will be clear and copious.

To be more specific, when your urine is clear, you're fine. When it starts turning yellow, you may be becoming dehydrated, and you should check your intake. When it is dark yellow, drink some water immediately.

To Be Fully Alive or Partially Dead

When my husband hands me a glass of water in the morning, he reminds me to drink it or be 2.5% dead. That's the percentage of body water he's estimated I've lost during the night. In our family, we take water intake seriously.

117

Dr. Wilkerson states that what made the difference in the Middle East Seven-Day-War was a difference of eight liters of water. As an example of the importance of water, he explains how the Israeli soldiers got better advice for fighting in the desert. They were forced to drink 10 liters (over 10 quarts) of water a day, while the Egyptians drank only their usual amount, 2 liters. Within very short time, the Egyptian army became exhausted, undoubtedly contributing to the early end of the war.

During the recent War in the Gulf much emphasis was put on seeing that our troops were well hydrated. In an article on health in *U.S News and World Report,* we were told that "[U.S. troops have] been exhorted by the brass to drink 3 gallons of water a day . . . to replace fluids lost in the 120-degree heat." Troops on maneuvers and in sand traps drank even more.

Measuring Individual Need

Fortunately we rarely are called upon to fight in the desert. So how can we know when a change in our environment or activity level changes our bodies' needs for water?

Obviously people have individual water needs—which will change throughout the life span—and the two-quart measure is only a starting point. It should be regularly reassessed through our internal mechanism to continually challenge and observe when we don't feel our best, or through watching the color of our urine. Under normal circumstances, however, we can feel confident that we're properly hydrated if we drink our personal equivalent of the two quarts of water.

But our individual needs can change at any time, in part because of what we are doing, where we are located, the weather, and whatever else we are experiencing. For example, we generally need more water in high altitudes, in hot climates, in the sun, and during periods of extreme humidity.

How much more water should you drink then? According to Dr. Wilkerson, just keep checking and drinking in the usual manner— that is, until your urine flows clear.

We also can look for other symptoms, in addition to generally just not feeling good. Some physical indicators of our body's urgent need for water are headaches, dizziness, mental confusion, physical clumsiness, general irritability, and a burning sensation upon urination.

EASTERN ASSOCIATION
WITH WATER

The yogis associate water with purification. There are many cleansing practices designed to clean and purify the inside as well as the outside of the body. According to the ancient system of Indian medicine (ayurveda), everything in nature comes from the five elements—earth, water, fire, air, and ether. They diagnose and treat people based on the amount of a certain element (in this case, water) there is in their system. And they also note how much water is available in the food they eat.

The Chinese system looks at the five elements in similar ways. The five elements listed in Chinese medicine are earth, water, fire, metal, and wood.

Besides the physical benefits listed earlier for water, Chinese medicine looks to the water element of the body to control emotions and regulate the very life force.

DINING WITH THE "INNER TEACHER" CAN BE FUN

Dining with the "Inner Teacher" can be an enjoyable and relaxing way to change dining habits. The *Health and Wholeness* students and I discovered that when we applied a body/mind/spirit perspective to our nutritional and water needs, we were able to bring a whole new light to this important health issue. We drew from the best of the contemporary knowledge of the West, while at the same time we explored the ancient wisdom of the East, and found we learned about ourselves in ways which not only benefited us, but also those around us.

RECOMMENDED NUTRITION AND WATER AWARENESS PROGRAM FOR HEALTH

FOR OPTIMAL HEALTH

1. Eat a diet high in complex carbohydrates, high in fiber, low in salt, low in sugar, low in fat, low in processed foods. This is essentially a diet rich in fresh vegetables, fresh fruits, and whole grains.

2. Drink two quarts of water per day (or whatever you have discovered is your optimal personal allotment). Drink enough water to keep your urine clear.

3. Notice what you eat, with whom you eat, and your attitude and emotions while you eat.

TO BEGIN

1. Make some small changes. For example, if you eat animal protein every meal, you may want to cut down on your intake, to reduce the fat and cholesterol you are taking into your body. Many people begin by making meat a side dish rather than their main entree. If you have a sweet tooth, try sweetening your food with frozen concentrated apple juice instead of sugar.

2. Increase your water intake by one glass per day for one week. Try drinking water different ways—hot, cold, and at room temperature. Start diluting your flavored beverages with more water. You can wean yourself from morning coffee or afternoon tea by first diluting their strength with warm water.

3. Think of ways to make your goals more fun. For instance, You can have "water parties" at your senior center or *Health and Wholeness* class. Offer water in fancy glassware or in china cups. You might try adding a lemon or an orange slice to your water (hot or cold) like they do in fancy restaurants.

PRECAUTIONS

Gradual rather than sudden changes in nutritional habits are recommended. Then the digestive organs and enzymes in the body have the time to adjust and accommodate to the work they need to do. And except for emergencies, the same is true of a sudden increase in doses of water. The cardiovascular and urinary systems may need time to adjust. A smooth transition to a healthier lifestyle allows for a smoother, more relaxing journey.

PERSONAL NUTRITION AND WATER GOALS

I will make the following changes in my diet for approximately _____ days, and notice how I feel.

_____

_____

I will increase my water intake by _____ ounces per day for _____ days, and notice how I feel.

I will drink enough water each day to keep my urine clear for _____ days, and notice how I feel.

I will engage my "Inner Teacher" by: _____

_____

_____

PROGRESS REPORT

Date

_____

What Done

_____

_____

_____

_____

Improvements Noticed

_____

_____

_____

_____

_____

_____

Reported to Whom

_____

FURTHER READING

THE WESTERN APPROACH

FINDLAY, Steven. "How to Bridge Your Water Gulf: Like the U.S. Troops, You May Need a Drink." *U.S. News and World Report* (October 22, 1990).

FRIES, James F. and Lawrence M. Crapo. *Vitality and Aging*. San Francisco: W. H. Freeman and Co., 1981.

GUSSOW, Joan Dye and Paul R. Thomas. *The Nutrition Debate: Sorting Out Some Answers*. Palo Alto, CA: Bull Publishing Co., 1986.

GUTHRIE, Helen Andres. *Introductory Nutrition*. St. Louis: C. V. Mosby Co., 5th ed., 1989.

LAMBERT-LAGACE, Louise. *The Nutrition Challenge for Women: Now You Don't Have to Diet to Stay Healthy and Fit*. Palo Alto, CA: Bull Publishing Co., 1990.

ORNISH, Dean. *Stress, Diet, and Your Heart*. New York: New American Library, 1983.

ORNISH, Dean. *Dr. Dean Ornish's Program for Reversing Heart Disease*. New York: Ballantine Books, 1992.

PELLETIER, Kenneth R. *Longevity: Fulfilling our Biological Potential*. New York: Dell Publishing Co., Inc., 1981.

SATTER, Ellyn. *How to Get Your Kid to Eat . . . But Not Too Much*. Palo Alto, CA: Bull Publishing Co., 1987.

WHITNEY, Eleanor Noss, Eva May Nunnelley Hamilton and Sharon Rady Folfes. *Understanding Nutrition*. St. Paul: West Publishing Co., 1990, 5th ed.

124

PART TWO

THE YOGIC APPROACH

BALLENTINE, Rudolph. *Diet and Nutrition: A Holistic Approach.* Honesdale, PA: The Himalayan International Institute, 1978.

SATCHIDANANDA, Sri Swami. *The Healthy Vegetarian.* Yogaville, VA: Integral Yoga Publications, 1986.

SATCHIDANANDA, Sri Swami. *Integral Yoga Teacher's Manual.* Yogaville, VA: Satchidananda Ashram, 1983.

THE CHINESE MEDICINE APPROACH

AUSTIN, Mary. *The Textbook of Acupuncture Therapy.* New York: Asi Publishers Inc., 1972.

CONNELLY, Diane. *Traditional Acupuncture: The Law of the Five Elements.* Columbia, MA: The Center for Traditional Acupuncture, Inc., rev. ed., 1979.

HAAS, Elson M. *Staying Healthy with the Seasons.* Berkeley, CA: Celestrial Arts, 1981.

125

❦

POINT FOUR

The Art of Relaxation

The soul that moves in the world of the senses and yet keeps
the senses in harmony . . . finds rest in quietness.

BHAGAVAD GITA

❦

Attain to the goal of absolute vacuity;
Keep to the state of perfect peace . . .
Going back to the origin is called peace . . .

TAO TE CHING
Chapter XVI

LESSON SIX
Progressive Deep Relaxation and Autogenic Relaxation

The ability to relax is our natural birthright. Babies have it, so do animals.

Let me brag a moment about T'Kope, our Samoyed sled dog. To T'Kope, relaxation is an honorable profession. She will lounge around our house all day, moving from one sunny spot to another without guilt or regret. But she is not lazy. All it takes is for someone to go for her leash, and she's up and ready for exercise.

Haven't you seen this with other animals? They can move from alert to relaxed states quite easily. Our neighbor's cat is even more amazing. When you hold her, every muscle in her body is relaxed. That is until T'Kope walks into the room. In a flash, she springs to action, jumping up on counters, hissing, scratching. But after the danger is over, back to sleep she goes.

WE CAN'T RELAX

Most of us lead active lives; if not physically busy, then mentally involved—always thinking, often worrying. Yet when we're ready to relax, to put it frankly, we can't. Our muscles tighten, our nerves tense, our minds remain in over-drive.

When heart patients come into my class, they can move their bodies, but they can't keep them still. When I teach them relaxation practices, they twist, they squirm. "How

127

can I possibly lie down for fifteen minutes each day," they complain, "I simply have too much to do."

My older students are not much better. They come to class complaining of what they know are stress-related disorders—spastic colons, headaches, tight muscle groups. Over three-quarters complain of sleeping poorly.

Some of my students require pills to go to sleep. Some require pills to wake them up. One day I asked my class to bring in all their prescription medication. There were so many bottles, some needed shoe boxes just to bring them to the session. "Does anyone have a Valium?" is no longer a joke. Tranquilizers, have become, just like coca-cola, a part of the American way of life.

Most sleeping pills and tranquilizers depress the nervous system. Amphetamines, in a sense, wake it up. Yet we need not rely on prescription drugs. Caffeine and alcohol have the same effect. Coffee in the morning can get us started and wine or brandy can put us to sleep.

But there is another option, one that regulates our nervous system through an internal control mechanism. And it requires no drugs. We can all learn ways to relax our muscles and calm and center our minds through natural means.

The rationale is quite simple: When the mind is tense, so is the body. On the other hand, when muscles relax, the mind can often relax as well.

I'll teach you several ways to relax *both* the body and the mind. But let me warn you. The difficulty is not in learning a practice. The challenge is in practicing it every day. In our society, we've gotten our nervous systems so out of shape, we must practice relaxation regularly just to keep our system in what should be its natural working order.

INTERNAL SOURCES OF RELAXATION

Every health practice presented in this book can lead to relaxation: deep three-part breathing, stretching slowly with awareness, exercising with an inward focus, and as mentioned in the previous chapter, even eating a proper diet. People often yawn in my class when deep breathing or doing the stretching. But instead of feeling insulted, I feel pleased. Relaxation is taking place.

There are many techniques for learning how to relax—progressive muscle deep relaxation, autogenic training, meditation, self-hypnosis, visualization (imagery). They all have something in common, a certain control they give us over our nervous system. Most important, they all mobilize our internal ability to relax naturally without the need to rely on external aids to relaxation.

PROGRESSIVE MUSCLE DEEP RELAXATION

By the end of this book you will have had some exposure to all of these relaxation techniques, but first I want to introduce progressive muscle deep relaxation. Sometimes called progressive muscle relaxation or simply progressive deep relaxation, this practice works at both the physical and the mental levels.

And in yogic terms, even other energy bodies can be reached. The final stage of relaxation in yoga is called "anandamyokosa," a long sanskrit word for something we all want to obtain, peace and bliss.

ITS MEDICAL APPLICATIONS

If you are not familiar with this progressive muscle relaxation, let me assure you that it has been accepted in American medical circles for years. Dr. Edmund Jacobson, a Chicago-based physician and physiologist, was one of the pioneers in this country to demonstrate the role that muscle tension and anxiety have played in disease.

He noticed back in the 30s that many of his patients had lost their ability to relax. In fact, he found that they even failed to recognize that certain muscles of theirs were chronically tense. Without this awareness they were unable to discern how to relax this tension.

So Dr. Jacobson sought out a method to teach them how. And for over fifty years physicians have used his book, *You Must Relax,* to treat patients with ulcers, tension headaches, high blood pressure, and other stress-induced illnesses.

Progressive muscle relaxation also became the basis for many child-birth breathing and relaxation exercises. It is often used to induce relaxation prior to hypnosis. And it has proved effective for use in other behavioral medicine therapies as well.

Interestingly enough, this treatment is quite similar to the relaxation practice recommended by yogis thousands of years ago. Often called "yoga nidra," this same type of relaxation continues to be taught in most hatha yoga classes around the world.

AN EXPLANATION AT THE BEGINNING

When I introduce this practice in my *Health and Wholeness* class, I explain at the beginning everything that I am going to say. This helps establish trust, and I've found that if people trust me and the process, they are more willing to allow themselves to let go, allowing relaxation to take place.

I break down my explanation into five steps:

Step I. *First, what I'm going to ask you to do is tense and then relax one muscle group at a time, from the feet to the head.* By tensing, even exaggerating your usual level of muscle tension, you will be able to notice what a contracted muscle feels like. Once you have this knowledge, you will be able to relax and release tension on your own.

This concept is important. Since most of us carry chronic tension in some part of our body most of the time, this contracted state must be pointed out to us, even exaggerated, so we can identify the feeling of muscle tension. Otherwise, we may think it's normal to walk around with our shoulders up to our ears. But once the relaxed state is also recognized, we are able to relax any muscle at will.

Step II. *Next, I'll ask you to relax each muscle group with your mind.* If you feel comfortable doing so, I'll ask that you close your eyes. This will help you focus *just* on a particular part of your body.

Step I and Step II help us develop appropriate body memory, a step toward learning neuro-muscular control. Once we have the body memory of what relaxation is, we can make our own corrections. Walking through town we can remind ourselves, "Shoulders feel tight . . . Relax the shoulder muscles."

Step III. *I'll explain how the practice teaches you to notice your breathing.* We've already discussed how the breath can release muscle tension. This time, however, we will not apply the deep three-part breath, but focus instead on our natural breathing pattern. By doing this for a full minute, we'll begin to learn the practice of observation.

If you're like most people, once you've tensed and relaxed muscles with your body, relaxed with your mind, then concentrated on your breathing, guess what happens? Your mind starts chattering:

"What am I going to have for dinner tonight?"

"Pasta with Marinara Sauce sounds good"

"Out of pasta . . . Need to go to the store."

"May not have enough cash to pay my grocery bill . . ."

And before you know it, your mind has tensed up your body again.

Step IV. *The practice teaches you to notice your thoughts as well.* I suggest to people that they watch their thoughts in the same way they watch T.V. The program will be your thoughts. The audience will be your observing self:

T.V. Program: "What am I going to have for dinner tonight?"

Audience: "That's interesting. Wonder what's going to happen next?"

T.V. Program: "Need to go to the grocery today."

Audience: "Hmm."

T.V. Program: "Probably won't have enough money to pay my bill . . ."

Audience: "That's interesting."

This practice of observing yourself is also a practice of detaching and becoming a witness. Notice a certain passive acceptance here. You are not criticizing yourself for needing to go to the store. You're not getting involved with the thought that you may not have enough money.

You most probably will have to deal with this situation later, but *not during relaxation.* During this part of the practice, all you are instructed to do is to watch and accept whatever thoughts come through. It's like watching clouds floating by.

Any time you feel yourself reacting to stress, you can immediately begin to observe yourself—which often reduces and may eliminate the beginning physiological reactions to stress.

Many religious orders feel this detachment process can foster an important spiritual experience. One can be "in the world, but not of the world." Shakespeare expresses it slightly differently: "All the world's a stage, And all the men and women merely players."

In the following text I will direct your awareness to different parts of your body. Instead of asking you to tense *your* right leg, for example, I'll refer to *the* right leg. This objective reference is done purposefully and consciously to further the detachment process during deep relaxation.

Getting this distance helps give us a different perspective about what might be happening inside our bodies as well as outside in our environment. This perspective and objective acceptance often brings with it a certain level of peace.

Step V. *There will be periods of silence after each section.* But after the last section, there will be extended silence for you to enjoy this deep peaceful and blissful state.

EXERCISE 6–1
THE PROGRESSIVE MUSCLE RELAXATION
PRACTICE

Deep relaxation usually works best at first if you have someone read the directions to you. Another way is to record your voice on a tape recorder and play it back for yourself.

Start by seating yourself comfortably in a chair. Or better yet, lie down on your bed or couch. Now listen to the following instructions read to you in a slow, relaxed pace. These come in substance from a typical Integral Yoga class:

"We'll be tensing different parts of the body, raising them a few inches and then, when the signal to release is given, just letting that part drop to the floor or surface.

Please bring the awareness to the right leg. Stretch it, tense the leg, raise it up, squeeze it tight . . . (*hold it approximately 5 seconds*) Relax. (Same with the left leg.) Gently roll the legs, if you wish, then forget about them.

Bring the awareness to the right arm. Stretch it out, stretch out the fingers. Now make a fist, raise the arm, squeeze it tight . . . (*for 5 seconds*) Relax. (Same with the left arm.)

Bring the awareness to the buttocks. Tense them; squeeze . . . (*a few seconds*) Relax. Feel the hips sinking down.

Bring the awareness to the abdominal area; inhale deeply through the nose, pushing the abdomen out like a balloon; hold the breath . . . Tighten the abdomen (*5 seconds*) . . . Open the mouth letting the air rush out, and the abdomen relaxes completely.

Bring the awareness to the chest. Inhale; expand the chest. Take in a little more air, still a little more . . . Hold the breath. (*5 seconds*) Open the mouth, letting the air rush out and the chest relax. Leaving the arms relaxed, bring the shoulders up toward the ears; then bring them together in front of the chest; then bring them down toward the toes. Relax.

Gently allow the head to roll from side to side, mentally relaxing the neck muscles. Return the head to center and relax.

Bring the awareness to the face. Gently move the jaw up and down . . . Relax. Squeeze the lips together in a pout . . . Relax. Suck in the cheeks . . . Relax. Wrinkle the nose, squint the eyes . . . Relax. Raise the eyebrows, wrinkle the forehead . . . Relax. Now squeeze all the muscles in the face to a point at the tip of the nose . . . Relax.

Now, without moving any part, begin going over the body mentally to relax any subtle tension. Begin bringing the awareness to the toes, feet, ankles, lower legs, knees, thighs, fingers, hands, wrists, forearms, elbows, upper arms, buttocks and pelvis, abdominal organs, rib cage, chest, lungs, heart and throat, lower back, middle back, upper back, shoulders, neck, jaw, tongue, lips, cheeks, nose, eyes, forehead, ears, sides of the head, back of the head, top of the head.

Now observe the body. Be the silent witness of the body, allowing it to be completely relaxed. (*5–10 seconds of silence*) Now observe the breath. Let it flow in and out by itself; just remain the witness. (*1 minute of silence*)

Now observe the mind and any thoughts that pass through it. Remain as the witness, without getting involved in the thoughts or images. (*1 minute of silence*)

Be aware of the peace within. This peace or the witness, is your True Self. Your True Nature is peace. Just feel the peace and enjoy that. Just feel the peace and enjoy that. (*5 full minutes of silence*)

Please bring the awareness back to the breath and observe its gentle flow. Gradually deepen the breath. (*Wait 30 seconds*) As the breath deepens imagine that fresh energy is gently entering into each part of the body, starting from the head downward . . . head, torso, arms, legs. The whole body is filled with vitality and fresh energy.'

Roll the head gently from side to side . . . roll the arms . . . and the legs. You may want to stretch and breathe deeply. Then slowly begin to open your eyes.

RELAXATION IS MORE THAN SLEEP

The yogis say fifteen minutes of deep relaxation provides the same benefit to the body as three hours of sleep. But deep relaxation is more than sleep. To obtain its full benefit you should *not* allow yourself to fall asleep during the practice. "Yoga nidra" means *conscious* sleep.

Have you noticed that when you wake up from sleep you often have a clenched jaw, a furrowed brow, stiff neck and shoulder muscles? Although sleep is beneficial and necessary for our health, it is not really effective in relieving life's tensions and stresses. Because a certain amount of physiological tension exists even during sleep, we need these relaxation techniques in addition to sleep to give us daily stress relief.

Exactly what is taking place? Dr. Herbert Benson did experiments to compare the relaxation response and sleep. He found differences in several areas. First, the need for oxygen is reduced in both situations, but with sleep this reduction is slow and progressive. Usually it takes four or five hours of sleep to lower one's oxygen needs 8% from one's waking state. During deep relaxation there is a 10–20% reduction within the first three minutes.

Have you noticed how stiff your muscles are in the morning when you awake? This is the result of lactic acid which has built up through skeletal muscle metabolism.

What is important for this discussion is the correlation between the amount of lactic acid in the blood and the degree of anxiety one feels. In contrast to the stiff after-effects of sleep, muscles tend to feel loose after deep relaxation, because there is no noticeable build up of lactic acid during deep relaxation.

Perhaps of even greater significance, however, are the research findings concerning the action of the brain during relaxation. If we were connected to an electroencephalogram machine (EEG), we could actually see what was happening with our brain.

Most of us spend our entire day in a beta state, which on an EEG recording looks something like this. During relaxation we move into a alpha or theta state. During sleep we are usually in a delta state.

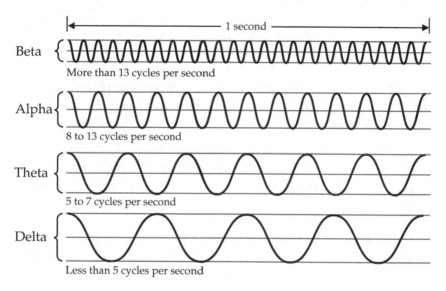

For reasons we do not fully know, alpha waves are present when people feel relaxed. And during an alpha brain wave state, the body is best able to heal itself. So when you learn a deep relaxation practice, you are learning a systematic way of entering this beneficial healing state.

139

DEEP RELAXATION:
THE TRUE MIRACLE DRUG

To me, deep relaxation is Mother Nature's miracle drug. We have now observed and others have recorded scientifically the miraculous benefits attainable through this practice. In a deep relaxed state we can: reduce our oxygen consumption, our carbon dioxide production, our heart rate, our respiration rate, and our production of lactic acid, while at the same time moving into an alpha-wave state. The net effect of these physiological changes is a reduction of activity in the sympathetic nervous system. The result is a healthy, restful state.

ANOTHER TECHNIQUE:
AUTOGENIC TRAINING

Some people argue against the progressive muscle relaxation technique. They feel it is unnecessary and even counterproductive to go through the alternate tensing and relaxing of muscles. The relaxation experts in this camp feel that once a muscle is contracted and metabolic activity is increased, it takes longer to get it back to a relaxed state again.

In Germany, psychiatrist J. H. Schultz and his student W. Luthe created "autogenic training," another way to obtain self-control over the sympathetic nervous system. Autogenic training uses only the mind to relax the body. Positive suggestions (or orientations) are given to induce a deep calm, restful state.

I usually start people with the Jacobson muscle tensing method, because most beginning students need to develop body awareness before they can relax individual muscle groups with the mind alone. However, as they progress (or if they have difficulty relaxing after contracting muscles), I give them this alternative.

The Six Orientations

Traditionally there are six basic orientations or positive suggestions (starting with the dominant side of your body):

1. "My right arm [or dominant arm] is very heavy."

2. "My right hand [or dominant hand] is warm."

3. "My pulse is calm and strong."

4. "My breath is calm and regular."

5. "My solar plexus is growing warm."

6. "My forehead is pleasantly cool."

These orientations are given and practiced one-at-a-time for a week or more. In autogenic training you must feel that your body has been trained and is responding to each suggestion before going on to the next.

If you want to add other parts of the body, do so, but it is recommended that you feel accomplished in the six basic orientations first. Within two months, if you practice each orientation regularly and in progression, you should be able to combine all six orientations and thereby master the complete physiologic effects expected from the autogenic method.

EXERCISE 6–2
AN AUTOGENIC RELAXATION PRACTICE

Here is a script I have developed for autogenic training. You will notice it takes you through all six orientations. Therefore, you will need to adapt it to where you are in your training. For example, if this is your first time, stop after you have experienced the heaviness in your dominant arm. Skip to the phrase, "I am at peace" and follow the ending. As you progress in your training, add each new orientation one-at-a-time.

Take some time to loosen your clothing and get yourself settled as comfortably as possible. You may want to pick a comfortable chair for sitting or you may want to lie down on a couch or bed.

Take a few deep breaths and allow your breathing to help you relax your body. You may want to close your eyes so you can focus more closely on deeply relaxing . . .

With each breath you can use a suggestion to take you deeper. As you inhale, you may want to repeat the phrase "I am." As you exhale, repeat the phrase "at peace." Continue to give yourself these instructions. (*Pause*) Feel your body respond.

Now focus on your right (or dominant) arm. Repeat the phrase "my arm is heavy." Say the phrase continuously until you experience a heavy feeling in this arm. (*Pause*) (*This is the first orientation.*)

When you are ready, begin to focus on the alternate arm. Again repeat the phrase "my arm is heavy."

Now add the phrase "my right (dominant) hand is warm." You might imagine that you have placed your hand in water, warm and comfortable to your touch. This warming of your hand is pleasurable and very peaceful. (*Pause*) (*This is the second orientation.*)

As your arms remain heavy and your dominant hand becomes warm, you might want to experience the other hand warming. Notice how comfortable and relaxed you have become. (*Pause*)

Now add the phrase "my pulse is calm and strong." You can imagine that the blood is flowing effortlessly throughout the body, nourishing every organ and every cell. (*Pause*)

Allow your mind to assist your body in this self-healing way. (*Pause*) (*This is the third orientation.*)

When you are ready, add the phrase "my breath is calm and regular." Say this over and over. Notice how your words deepen and calm your breath. (*Pause*) (*This is the fourth orientation.*)

As the blood flows throughout the body, repeat the phrase, "my solar plexus is growing warm." Notice how you can bring it to the temperature that is comfortable for you. (*Pause*) (*This is the fifth orientation.*)

Now notice the forehead. Feel how relaxed it has become. Add the phrase, "my forehead is pleasantly cool." Experience your entire being as relaxed and very calm. (*Pause*) (*You have completed the sixth orientation.*)

When ready return to the original phrase, "I am at peace." With each inhale repeat the words "I am." With each exhale repeat the words "at peace." Continue. (*Pause*)

Feel the sense of well-being and calmness you have established. Through your own suggestions you have transformed your body in the direction of its own *health and wholeness*.

Now slowly bring your awareness to the room. You may want to stretch or yawn. And when you are ready, slowly open your eyes.

LESSON SEVEN
Acupressure for Pain Relief and Relaxation

When you've relearned the art of relaxation as you experienced it as a baby, you have a powerful key to peace of mind. But, many of my students have difficulty going directly to relaxation practices if they are experiencing severe pain from arthritis or extreme muscle tension. It's just too difficult to concentrate on relaxation when the mind is focused on pain. So, I also teach acupressure for pain relief and relaxation.

Acupressure and acupuncture have been used for some 5,000 years. The ancient Chinese discovered pressure points near the surface of the skin that relieved pain by increasing the circulation and balancing the body's life force.

Some acupressure points were discovered by accident. For instance, Dr. Stephan Chang in *The Complete Book of Acupuncture* suggests,

> *In the dawn of history when stones and arrows were the only implements of war, many soldiers wounded on the battlefield reported that symptoms of disease that had plagued them for years had suddenly vanished. Naturally such strange occurrences baffled the physicians who could find no logical relationships between the trauma and the ensuing recovery of health. Finally after many years of meticulous observation it was concluded that certain illnesses could actually be cured by striking or piercing specific points on the surface of the body.*

Through our natural instincts, we do acupressure on ourselves all the time. Don't you instinctively hold the part of your body that aches or hurts? The ancient Chinese, I believe, just paid attention to what they did intuitively and noticed when they got results. They used their "Inner Teacher" and developed an effective system that has been passed down for thousands of years.

One thing they observed was that when energy was blocked, a person experienced pain or illness. They soon learned to discover these blockages by identifying places on the body that tended to be tense and constricted. By releasing the tension at these points along the energy meridians, they reopened the pathways for this energy to flow.

Over 700 points have been charted and passed down from generation to generation. With the use of a machine called a galvanometer, Western physicians have discovered that there are certain areas on the skin that have less electrical resistance. These areas have been found to coincide with those points recorded by the Chinese thousands of years ago.

When pressure is properly applied to these points it is called *acupressure.* In other words, we are using finger pressure to relieve tension and pain. When you go to a practitioner who uses needles in these points, the therapy is called *acupuncture.*

The points used in acupressure and acupuncture are the same. In fact, you could also have heat applied to these points through a method called "moxa", or have sound applied through the use of a tuning fork. Later I'll share with you some other options my students have devised.

HOW TO GET RELIEF THROUGH ACUPRESSURE

For several years now I have included acupressure training in my classes. Even when students have been unable to reconcile Eastern philosophy with their faith in traditional Western medicine, they have enjoyed learning about the practice and its tradition. Others have found it brought tangible improvements in their health.

For the relief of pain, especially pain from arthritis, it is important to do more than hold acupressure points. In my own acupressure training I was told that stretching exercises (like those taught in an earlier chapter) are important for moving energy along meridian lines. When you hold the points, you must breathe deeply. Getting blood to the point is important. Getting fully oxygenated blood does even more. Deep breathing also keeps you relaxed while you are in the learning phase of this practice.

"How long should I hold the point?" I'm always asked. A trained acupressurist would hold the point until he or she felt an energy pulse. The energy pulse feels much like the blood pulse you experience when you hold your wrist.

Because beginning students may not have developed enough finger sensitivity to feel energy pulses, or because they get too discouraged waiting for the energy to move, I suggest counting breaths instead. If you hold a point and take five, long, deep three-part breaths, you will hold the point long enough to get positive effects.

ACUPRESSURE BRINGS RELAXATION

As we discussed early in the book, the goal of treatment in Chinese medicine is not symptom relief but bringing the

147

energy of the body into balance. For this reason, no matter what symptoms may prompt a patient to seek out an acupressure practitioner (lower back pain, arthritis, migraines, etc.), there often are side benefits such as deep relaxation and better sleep patterns.

This chapter is concerned with the art of relaxation, and the following acupressure points do promote a restful and balanced state. However, I have also selected points that relate specifically to particular problems students have brought to class, as well as ones that we can reach and hold easily.

RELAXING WHILE HOLDING POINTS

Like any other practice, during the learning phase, we can create stress for ourselves while we are trying to reduce it. Holding acupressure points can create tension in our bodies, unless we consciously relax as we hold them.

Effective ways to do this include breathing while holding points, and moving the arms and fingers as you breathe. Or between points, gently shake out the fingers, arms, or any other part of your body that may be stiff.

Usually students use the pads of their fingers to hold the points, but there are no concrete rules. Anything that provides gentle stimulation to these points will work.

Some of my students with severe arthritis in their fingers have found it painful to hold points the usual way. They improvised with the eraser end of a pencil. One student with severe bursitis couldn't reach the shoulder and neck points. So, she used the crook in her umbrella. For the neck and shoulder points, some people lie on folded socks or use soft foam balls. I sometimes tape magnets to points on my skin I want to work.

I use the traditional Chinese names and the actual meridian point numbers for those who are interested in pursuing this Chinese healing system further. But don't feel that you need to remember these names or labels. The results you receive from holding the points are what is important.

EXERCISE 7–1
ACUPRESSURE FOR BETTER HEALTH

FIVE POINTS ON THE HANDS AND ARMS

HOKU (Large Intestine 4)

Location: Highest spot of the muscle when the thumb and the index finger are brought close together. Press firmly into the webbing between the thumb and index finger.

Benefit: Used to relieve arthritis in all parts of the body, particularly in the hands, wrists, elbows, and shoulders. Also is said to relieve constipation, headaches, toothaches, lower jaw problems, common cold, insomnia. It moves energy downward.

FISH REGION (Lung 10)

Location: On the palm side of the hand in the center of the big mound at the base of the thumb. Press toward the bone.

Benefit: Relieves arthritis in the hand, coughing, swollen throat, upset stomach, anorexia, allergies, and assists general pain control.

150

INNER GATE (Pericardium 6)

Location: Two finger widths from the wrist crease, between the ulna and radius, on the inside of the arm.

Benefit: Relieves nausea, hiccoughs, shock, dizziness, insomnia.

OUTER GATE (Triple Warmer 5)

Location: Two finger widths from the wrist flexure, between the ulna and the radius, on the outside of the arm.

Benefit: Relieves pain in wrist, arms and shoulders, stiff neck, toothache, headaches, common cold, flu.

CROOKED POND (Large Intestine 11)

Location: In the elbow joint at the outer end of the crease where arm bends.

Benefit: Relieves joint inflammation, particularly in the elbow and shoulder joints. Lowers blood pressure. Builds immune system. Relieves sore throat and constipation.

THREE POINTS FOR THE BACK AND NECK

HEAVENLY BONE (Triple Warmer 15)

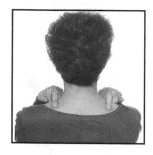 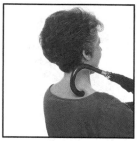

Location: Little hollow just above the tip of scapula bone on the back. Reach your hand over your shoulder, curving your fingers. Hook on-to the trapezius muscle on the top of your shoulders. Let the weight of your arms hold the point as you lower them toward the front of your body. (You can choose to use the crook of your umbrella or walking cane.)

Benefit: Relieves shoulder and neck stiffness, pain, including rheumatism. Lowers fever. Builds immune system.

EXTRA LOVELY (Extra Point Not Traditionally Given a Number)

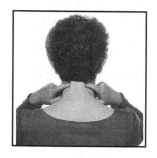

Location: Halfway down the neck, one thumb's width outside the spine. Usually a lump of muscle tension can be felt on one or both sides. Press toward the spine.

Benefit: Relieves stiffness, rigidity, and arthritis pain in the neck and back. Benefits nervous system. Relieves stress.

WIND POND (Gall Bladder 20)

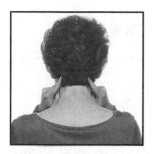

Location: Hollow below the base of the skull in between two muscles on either side of the spine. Apply slight pressure and massage.

Benefit: Relieves arthritic pain, headaches, hypertension, insomnia, back pain, eyestrain, stiff neck, irritability, nervousness, mental pressures, dizziness, rheumatism. Improves memory.

EXERCISE 7–2
ESPECIALLY TO CALM AND RELAX

There is an energy line, called the Conception/ Governing Vessel, that runs down the midline of the front of the body and up the back. I always hold points along this line to deepen the relaxation effect at the end of an acupressure session. I also use it when a client is extremely agitated. My *Health and Wholeness* students who suffer from insomnia tell me these points have been especially helpful to them.

DIRECTIONS

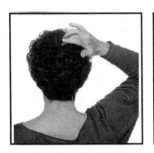  Place your third finger of your right hand on the crown of your head in between the cranial bones. You may feel a slight hollow or soft spot slightly behind the top of the head. The ancient Chinese call it *ONE HUNDRED MEET-ING POINT (Governing Vessel 20),* since they believe that 100 energy channels meet at this point.

Keeping your right hand in position, now place the third finger of your left hand in the midline between the eyebrows *(THE THIRD EYE— Governing Vessel Between 24 and 25).* Take at least five deep three-part breaths.

Still keeping your right hand in position, bring your left hand to the center of the sternum, at the level of the heart and hold this point in the same manner. Continue the deep breathing as described above.

This last point is called the *SEA OF TRANQUILITY (Conception Vessel 17).* It is one of the most calming points on the body. It is good for balancing the emotions—anxiety, fear, loneliness, grief, depression. The Chinese say it benefits the cardiovascular system by nourishing the heart and opening up the breathing.

Place the left palm between the pubic bone and the navel. Bring the right palm to rest gently on the right hand. *(THE SEA OF ENERGY—Conception Vessel 6)* Breathe deeply into this area and feel your abdominal muscles expand and contract.

This area is called the "hara," a key area for the development of energy, power and centeredness. This point strengthens the abdominal muscles, intestines, and the uro-genital system. This point is said to help us find our balance and place in the world.

155

THE MENTAL AND SPIRITUAL
APPROACH TO RELAXATION

Deep relaxation is a body/mind technique. One cannot achieve a relaxed state unless *both* the body is relaxed and the mind is calmed. However many people do not realize that relaxation involves a form of spiritual practice too. Every religion I've studied instructs its followers to quiet themselves. Some version of "Be still and know I am God."

For those who ascribe to no formal religious orientation, I remind them that the peace we feel during deep relaxation is our natural self, our core, our center. To me, discovering this core is more than a matter of just physical health. We are connecting more deeply with our own essence.

GIVING AWAY RELAXATION

To enhance the spiritual aspect of this practice, I encourage you to give it away. When a friend is ill or anxious, offer to lead him through a deep relaxation practice. Or make and send him a tape recording of one. Most likely something wonderful will happen.

I have yet to guide someone into a deep relaxed state without getting deeply relaxed myself. When I teach other health topics, I'm often tired when class is over. I've expended energy and my body knows it. But when I teach deep relaxation to others, the regenerating experience returns to me. I always leave a class or session feeling renewed, replenished and full of energy.

HOW TO GIVE RELAXATION AWAY

When leading someone through deep relaxation, use your voice consciously. Speak very slowly and compassionately, with a lot of silence between sections. Words, too often, keep us in a beta brain wave state. Silence moves us more into the alpha state.

Soothing meditation music may help to slow down your speaking rhythm. But be sure that your partner likes your music selection and is not distracted by it. The volume is important too, not so loud as to compete with your instructions. Not so soft as to make him strain to hear.

HOW TO GIVE ACUPRESSURE AWAY

If you want a friend for life, offer to give a person you like a back rub. You can do it with your friend sitting in a chair or lying down. Do whatever feels comfortable to your body as well as your partner's.

EXERCISE 7–3
GIVING ACUPRESSURE AWAY

Directions: Before you begin, take some deep breaths. Ask your friend to do this also. Relaxation takes the acupressure deeper. Decide whether the two of you want music.

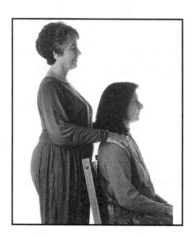

Position your body, so that you are absolutely comfortable. No reason to hurt yourself while helping someone else.

Now let your fingers do the walking. Begin to rub in any way that feels good to your friend and doesn't hurt you. You can use your fingers, your palm, your knuckles, your arms, or any part of your body. (The Chinese have been known to do a wonderful massage called barefoot shiatsu, using—you guessed it—their feet.) Ask your partner what amount of pressure she likes. Move with your whole body, like a dance—with smooth, easy movements.

Whenever you are ready to do so, you can begin to hold the acupressure points listed earlier (first, HEAVENLY BONE (shoulder muscles), then, EXTRA LOVELY (neck muscles,) and finally, WIND POND (under the skull line). You can hold one or both sides. You can hold them simultaneously, or one at a time.

The main instruction is just like that given for deep relaxation go slowly and with compassion. This time you're speaking with your fingers instead of your voice.

When it is time to end, ease off slowly. I like to tap my partner gently or give some other non-verbal message that I'm about ready to stop. When possible, suggest that the person rest quietly for a while. Most acupressurists recommend that for maximum benefit a client should schedule at least an hour of relaxation after an hour of acupressure.

But how does giving away these practices lead to spiritual health? To be present with your friend in this way is to connect with her at a very deep level. Just like when teaching deep relaxation, when giving an acupressure session, energy can be exchanged.

But you get something extra, as well. My students who have arthritis in their hands and wrists have found that the best exercise to relieve their pain is to give someone else a massage.

So you might just ask your partner to return the favor. Then both of you get the pleasure of receiving a back rub and the relief from arthritic pain when giving one back.

RELAXATION IS A SPIRITUAL PRACTICE

I've listened to people ask their spiritual teachers serious questions: "Should I get a divorce?" "Should I move in with my children?" "Which cancer treatment should I accept?"

The questions are different, the life stresses not the least bit alike. Accordingly, the advice has come with different words.

But when I've listened closely, there is a similarity to the response. What these religious leaders all seem to advise is some form of: "Do what you need to do to maintain your inner peace."

T'Kope was right after all. Relaxation *is* an honorable profession and a spiritual practice as well.

RECOMMENDED RELAXATION PROGRAM
FOR HEALTH

FOR OPTIMAL HEALTH

1. Practice some deep relaxation technique for 15 minutes each day. This could be the progressive deep relaxation or the autogenic one.

2. Practice some acupressure preventively every day.

TO FEEL BETTER

1. Start noticing where you are carrying tension in your body, and relieve it by relaxing that particular part of the body, as in Step I and II of Progressive Deep Relaxation or through the Autogenic Training.

2. Notice when your thoughts create areas of tension in your body, and release them through the "art of observing and detaching," as instructed in Step IV of Progressive Deep Relaxation.

3. Relieve pain and discomfort through the use of specific acupressure points.

PRECAUTIONS

If you take medication for heart problems or epilepsy, you may want to have them near by. Although deep relaxation is extremely beneficial for both conditions, those very sensitive to changes in the nervous system have been known to have physiological responses.

161

When giving yourself or someone else an acupressure session, be sure to keep your body relaxed in the ways outlined earlier. If you are relaxed, you cannot hurt yourself or others from holding the wrong point, holding it too long, or in the wrong way. And you need only hold points on one side of the body. In Chinese tradition, when the energy is released, it goes to both sides automatically.

Since HOKU brings energy downward, observe the Chinese caution against using it on pregnant women, except during labor.

PERSONAL RELAXATION GOALS

I will do the following the following deep relaxation practice for _____ minutes each day and notice how I feel:

_____ Progressive Deep Relaxation

_____ Autogenic Relaxation

I will hold the following acupressure points on myself each day and notice how I feel:

Points on Hands and Arms

___ Hoku

___ Fish Region

___ Inner Gate

___ Outer Gate

___ Crooked Pond

Points on Back and Neck

___ Heavenly Bone

___ Extra Lovely

___ Wind Pond

Calming and Relaxing Routine

___ One Hundred Meeting Point

___ Third Eye

___ The Sea of Tranquility

___ The Sea of Energy

Growing Older *Feeling Better*

P R O G R E S S   R E P O R T

Date

_____

What Done

_____

_____

_____

_____

Improvements Noticed

_____

_____

_____

_____

_____

_____

Reported to Whom

_____

FURTHER READING

RELAXATION TECHNIQUES

BENSON, Herbert. *The Relaxation Response.* New York: William Morrow and Co., Inc., 1975.

BENSON, Herbert. *Beyond the Relaxation Response.* New York: Berkley Books, 2nd ed., 1985.

BORYSENKO, Joan. *Minding the Body, Mending the Mind.* New York: Bantam Books, 1988.

CRISWELL, Eleanor. *How Yoga Works: An Introduction to Somatic Yoga.* Novato, CA: Freeperson Press, 1989.

JACOBSON, Edmund. *You Must Relax.* 4th ed. New York: McGraw-Hill, 1962.

JAFFE, Dennis T. *Healing From Within: Psychological Techniques to Help the Mind Heal the Body.* New York: Simon and Schuster, Inc., rev. ed., 1980.

SCHULTZ, J.J. and W. Luthe. *Autogenic Therapy.* New York: Grune & Stratton, 1969.

SATCHIDANANDA, Sri Swami. *Integral Yoga Teachers' Training Manual.* Yogaville, VA: Satchidananda Ashram, 1983.

VISHNU Devananda, Swami. *The Sivananda Companion to Yoga: A Complete Guide to the Physical Posture, Breathing Exercises, Diet, Relaxation and Mediation Techniques of Yoga.* New York: A Fireside Book, 1983.

ACUPRESSURE

CHANG, Stephan. *The Complete Book of Acupressure.* Millbrae, CA: Celestial Arts, 1976.

165

GACH, Michael Reed. *Acupressure's Potent Points: A Guide to Self-Care for Common Ailments.* New York: Bantam Books, 1990.

GACH, Michael Reed. *Acu-Yoga: The Acupressure Stress Management Book.* New York: Japan Publications, 1981.

GACH, Michael Reed. *Arthritis Relief at Your Fingertips: The Complete Self-Care Guide to Easing Aches and Pains Without Drugs.* New York: Warner Books, 1989.

GACH, Michael Reed. *Arthritis Relief At Your Fingertips: Morning and Evening Routines.* Acupressure Institute, 1533 Shattuck Ave, Berkeley, CA. 94709 (Audio Tape)

PENDLETON, Bonnie and Betty Mehling. *Relax! With Self-Therap/Ease: A Simple Illustrated Course.* Englewood Cliffs, N.J.: Prentice-Hall, Inc., 1984.

TEEGUARDEN, Iona Marsaa. *Acupressure Way of Health: Jin Shin Do.* New York: Japan Publications, 1978.

POINT FIVE

Maintaining a Focused Mind and a Positive Attitude

The wind turns a ship
From its course upon the waters:
The wandering winds of the senses
Cast man's mind adrift
And turn his better judgment from its courses
When a man can still his senses
I call him illumined.

BHAGAVAD GITA

For as he thinketh in his heart, so is he.

THE BIBLE
Proverbs 23:7

LESSON EIGHT
Positive Imagery

Did you know you could actually scare yourself to death? It's the truth. Dr. Robert Eliot, while at the University of Nebraska, began studying people who died suddenly and unexpectedly. Until his study, most of such people were thought to have died from an unexplained cardiac arrest. But Dr. Eliot found that in most cases a chemical had been released in the body prior to the heart attack. In other words some stimulus (probably anxiety or fear) had released a chemical that triggered the body's reaction and subsequent death.

We scare ourselves all the time. We can expect to have some type of physiological response any time we are afraid, anxious, angry, even worried (unless we are able to put into practice techniques such as those described in this book). These responses can sometimes be life-saving (e.g., when we need to fight or flee). But too often they can wear us down and cause all kinds of ailments, even premature death.

MEDICAL CRISIS AND THE MIND

Let me tell you what happened to me as I wrote the first draft of this chapter. I had been in the Marble Mountain Wilderness of Northern California for five days alone on a Vision Quest. (This is a Native American custom observed during major rites of passage, or whenever the individual feels the need to spend some quiet time with "the Great Spirit.")

168

Although there are many variations of the tradition, my husband and I were under the tutelage of Red Hawk, a medicine man from the Karuk tribe. Red Hawk believes that the Quest is between the "quester" and the "Great Spirit." In other words, under his leadership Red Hawk does not find it necessary to set external rules, safety regulations or established time limits for the solo experience.

So off I went alone to a spot of my choice in the wilderness, without a tent, taking but two liters of water and a small amount of food—four oranges and four granola bars. The idea was to make myself vulnerable to nature and to listen for spiritual guidance. My guidance was clear. On the afternoon of the fifth day, I should return.

So when the last day came, I was prepared. I finished my last few bites of granola and the last segments of orange; I had rationed my food and water just right.

But as I was moving around my site, I carelessly slipped and all my weight went down on the outside of my right foot which, unfortunately, was pressed against a large granite rock.

As my foot began to swell, I sat in denial. "This just couldn't be happening to me." But as I tried to walk, I realized it undoubtedly had. My right foot could not bear my weight without severe pain.

"How will I get to base camp?" "No one will know I've been hurt." My thoughts came quickly now that reality set in. Our group was not scheduled to leave the mountains for four more days. Thinking it through, I realized I might not even be missed until then.

"I have no food," I reminded myself. Then I thought of something worse. "I'm almost out of water and I can't get down the steep hill to the closest spring." I was really scaring myself now, so, of course, I took it further. "Even if they find me, I'll never be able to walk in this condition— not for a two-day hike out of the mountains."

A full-blown panic attack was in progress. And my stress level was rapidly increasing. My quest might be over; but my survival had just begun.

Then I looked at myself and laughed. Here I was doing everything I teach others NOT to do. It was time to apply my own principles. My foot was still swollen, I was in the same mess, but somehow my stress reduction program was coming into practice. In the way we discussed deep relaxation earlier, I began to view my thoughts as a program on television that I was merely watching. Immediately my reactions turned from panic to entertainment.

T.V. Program: "I'm panicking."

Audience: "That's interesting."

T.V. Program: "Now I'm laughing at myself."

Audience: "This could be entertaining."

"Take three deep breaths," (I began to teach myself right from my own lesson plans.) "Now give yourself some positive messages."

I reminded myself that I was trained in first aid, I had survival skills, and I happened to love this beautiful meadow where I now had been for five days. I was just going to have a longer stay than I'd expected, that's all.

170

The next thing I did was assess the injury. Probably a badly bruised or slightly cracked metatarsal bone, I diagnosed. "Make a splint with your red bandanna and elevate the foot to relieve swelling." My first aid knowledge was returning. I kept reminding myself that at this moment I was fine, and all I had to do was stay calm.

I could even image my foot perfectly healed, and being able to walk out of my campsite with ease. But just in case, I put in some other images. I saw myself riding out of the Marbles on horseback or enjoying the experience of a helicopter rescue.

And as it was, I was discovered the next day. When my friends found me I was laughing—just thinking about this chapter I was going to write about keeping a positive attitude during medical crisis.

VISUALIZING HEALTH

To stay healthy, especially during difficult times, one must train the mind to visualize health promoting images. Western physicians know that "the will-to-live" can pull many people right through life-threatening illnesses. In a similar way, "the will-for-health" can help us through many difficult situations.

Western medicine has demonstrated how this works, by challenging visualization and other mental techniques with rigorous scientific testing. And like Dr. Eliot, they are finding a chemical basis for these "miraculous" recoveries.

They involve a number of chemicals, called neuropeptides, which are manufactured in the brain. Some are produced by white blood cells. Since they directly affect how we feel, they're often referred to as "molecules of emotions."

171

Have you noticed that just remembering a special occasion with a close friend or loved one makes you feel good all over. It's as if the event is actually happening again, with all its good feelings.

On the other hand, have you noticed how miserable you can make yourself feel by just recalling some bad experience? Dr. Martin L. Rossman, the author of *Healing Yourself: A Step-By-Step Program For Better Health Through Imagery*, reminds us that if we can be affected emotionally to get sick, so we can systematically use our emotions to get ourselves well.

BODY/MIND STUDIES: PSYCHONEUROIMMUNOLOGY

Each of us has stories from our own life or from the lives of others that demonstrate the effect of the mind on the body. However, most medical scientists would pay little attention to your experience, even if it saved your life. Unless personal experiences, no matter how important or incredible, are subject to rigorous experimentation, they are not taken seriously.

Anecdotes may be considered "interesting" by scientists, but since they rarely are subjected to the rigors of standard experimentation protocols (with experimental and control groupings, for example), the lessons of the stories cannot be applied generally to other people or situations. They are, therefore, viewed as scientifically valueless.

But within the past ten years a whole field of study, called psychoneuroimmunology, has begun to draw medical attention. Noted scientists such as Joan Borysenko, Caroline Hellman, Matthew Budd and Herbert Benson of the Harvard Medical School have begun to study seriously the effect of the body/mind phenomena.

VISUALIZATION AND THE IMMUNE SYSTEM

One study by Drs. Janice Kiecolt-Glaser and Ron Glaser of Ohio State University looks at the effect of imagery on the immune systems of older adults.

Medical science knows that the effectiveness of the immune system declines with age. This might explain why flu and cancer rates are higher for older people. The Glasers' wanted to see if they could revitalize the immune system of older people, through the use of relaxation and visualization techniques.

So they took forty-five healthy seniors who lived in a retirement home in Columbus, Ohio, and placed them into three groups. One group (experimental group A) was taught relaxation and imagery skills by medical students. To rule out the possibility that the social contact with the students rather than the relaxation and imagery skills was causing an effect, another group (experimental group B) received social visits from the students, but no training in the body/mind techniques. Another group (the control group) had neither training nor visits.

The results were impressive. Group A, the group that was taught relaxation and visualization, showed an increase in number of white blood cells, the cells that actually kill off invading viruses and bacteria. In addition, Group A measured lower resting heart rates, lower breathing rates, and less perspiration. They also reported feeling more relaxed and confident than the other subjects in the study. Finally, they reported that they were thinking more clearly and, in general, feeling more control over their lives.

VISUALIZATION TO WORK WITH
PAIN AND SUFFERING

Medical centers across the country are beginning to understand the possibilities of imagery for healing, but this acceptance hasn't come easily. Although imagery has always been used to some degree by healers in all cultures, only recently have Western physicians begun to pay attention. They have no longer been able to ignore cases where patients with serious problems (who have experienced no relief from continuous traditional treatments) have received immediate relief from "nontraditional" and "unorthodox" ones.

This has been especially true in cases of sufferers from chronic pain. "Many doctors tend to think of pain as a *thing*," says Dr. David Bresler, the former director of the UCLA Pain Control Unit and currently the executive director of the Bresler Center Medical Group in Santa Monica, California. "So they'll block the nerve that's carrying that *thing* with an anesthetic, or they'll even cut the nerve."

Dr. Bresler explains how doctors will do this with medicines too. "If it hurts a little [they] give the patient an aspirin, if it hurts a little more [they] give aspirin with codeine, a little more [they] give Demerol. If those don't work, many doctors tell the patient it's hopeless and he'll have to learn to live with the constant pain."

What does Bresler think of this type of medical treatment and attitude? "I consider that view shocking and irresponsible."

Pain reduction, according to Bresler, can be reached through other means. He uses hypnosis, biofeedback, acupuncture, relaxation exercises, acupressure massage, nutritional counseling, marital and family counseling, *and* visualization.

Dr. Martin Rossman, an internist from Mill Valley, California, is one of the growing number of physicians trained in Western medicine who have begun using imagery techniques in their medical practices. When Dr. Rossman was practicing traditional medicine, he saw hundreds of patients come and go—and not get well. Then he learned a way to help patients look at pain, suffering, and disease from the perspective of the patient's personal experience. To do this, he used visualization.

Along with Bresler and Rossman, others who have led the way, combining imagery practices with Western medical techniques include Drs. Carl and Stephanie Matthews-Simonton, with their pioneering work with cancer patients in Texas; Dr. Norman Shealy with his work at the Pain Rehabilitation Center in Wisconsin; Dr. Jeanne Achterberg and Dr. Frank Lawlis, with their early work at the Burn Unit of the University of Texas Health Science Center in Dallas.

Although their work differed in some degree, they all used forms of relaxation and imagery. They also insisted that success with these practices was the result of enhancing the internal mechanism of healing available naturally to each of their patients.

HOW IS VISUALIZATION DONE?

There are many techniques, but they all have the following in common:

1. *The image chosen should be pleasurable and soothing to the individual.* When at all possible, even when leading groups I try to have students pick their own colors, scenes, and experiences. Carl and Stephanie Simonton learned that effective imagery is a highly individual matter. What works for one person is not right for another.

In the beginning, they had all their cancer patients work with the image of "pac-men" eating up cancer cells. However, while some patients took to this aggressive image readily, others responded to it poorly. They therefore changed the instructions to give patients freedom to select their own images.

2. *Imagery can use one or a combination of the senses.* Some people feel they must see the image for it to work. That's what the word visualization means to them. But not all people are oriented visually. Some people hear, taste, smell and/or feel their image. In groups I often use the word "experience" instead of "see," "hear," or "feel," so people know they can choose which sense works for them.

3. *The image must be presented positively and must be enjoyable.* Every time we worry, we're visualizing. Since we all can worry so well, the challenge isn't simply to visualize. It is to change the negative imagery, with its unhealthy physiologic responses, to positive imagery, with its subsequent healthy ones.

In my camping situation, I had begun the negative process. I saw myself starving, undiscovered, unable to walk out of the mountains. These were unhealthy images that were feeding my panic. When the mind is allowed free reign in a threatening situation, fear and anxiety usually take over. I was only moments away from seeing buzzards swirling around my head.

I had to take control of my mind and replace the negative messages with positive ones. When I did, it raised my confidence level, so that I could believe in a positive outcome. Instead of seeing my lonely death, I chose to see my foot completely healed and a successful return to my companions.

But in crisis, one usually has a "yes, but" response. In my case I convinced myself I would be found and my foot would eventually heal, but I still didn't believe my bone could completely heal itself in four days. So I continued to worry about not being able to walk out of the mountains on my wounded foot. To deal with this fear, I saw myself enjoying riding horseback out of the mountains or being thrilled by a helicopter rescue.

I was taking the conservative route. A skilled and extremely confident visualizer might have felt she had the power to completely heal the bone in a matter of days; for this person, the first image of a healed foot might have been enough. I felt I wanted contingency plans, so I added the rescue scenarios. Any one of my visualized outcomes might have worked, if my belief system had been strong enough to support my image.

But there is another important point. The imaging experience must not only be positive, but also enjoyable. For example, if I had been afraid of horses or embarrassed by a rescue effort, neither of those visual experiences would have been helpful to me.

177

We thus can see how each person must choose what is positive and enjoyable for him or her. What might be highly effective for one person could be devastating for another. To reemphasize, imagery must be highly personal.

4. *The image should be optimal and set in the present period of time.* Although there are different philosophies here, I prefer to strive for the optimal health image in the here and now. For instance with heart patients, I suggest that they see their arteries wide and open (not just getting wider), and that they feel their heart beat strong and regular (not just getting stronger and more regular).

I look at it this way: Since we are in control of creating our imagery experience, we might as well aim high and see ourselves having already arrived at our healthiest goals.

LESSON NINE
The One-Two Punch: Visualization and Meditation

People who are most effective in creating change through imagery are those best able to relax and also best able to focus their minds. This is why visualization is usually taught in conjunction with meditation.

In Dr. Herbert Benson's early work he found that those people who could meditate required less oxygen, gave off less carbon dioxide, were able to lower both their breathing and their heart rates, and had lower blood pressure. They also had less lactic acid in their blood and more alpha and theta brain waves. In other words, they exhibited the same effects associated with deep relaxation. The meditators had reversed the stress response.

When meditation is used in connection with visualization, I call it "the one-two punch." Dr. Dean Ornish compares it to focusing sun rays through a magnifying glass so that the rays can become strong enough to start a fire. In a similar way our imagery becomes more focused and strong.

HOW DO YOU MEDITATE?

There are many forms of meditation—some quite esoteric, others quite mundane. I've seen people meditate, whether they called it that or not, while gardening, swimming laps, sitting in front of a fire, watching a sun set. Anything that focuses your mind inward, and reaches a point where you feel more whole and connected can be, I believe, meditation.

179

The way to know for sure is to ask yourself this question: Do I feel more relaxed, calm, and connected because of this experience?

FOUR STEPS FOR MEDITATION

When asked to teach meditation, I usually use Dr. Benson's method, because of its simplicity. He only includes four steps.

1. *Sit quietly.* Use a straight chair so your spine can remain erect. Now try to keep the body perfectly still.

2. *Close the eyes.* This is not always necessary, but in the beginning states it helps to keep out visual distractions.

3. *Repeat a word, sound, thought or image.* What you choose is not important as long as it is uplifting to you. Some people choose the word "peace." Some people like to hear the sound of the ocean or the sound of their own breath. Some people like to hold the image of the petals of a favorite flower. If you feel comfortable with a repetitive prayer, its use can be very effective.

Experiment at first, but once you've found what works best for you, stay with it. With repeated use, you will find you are increasingly able to discipline your mind and build up your body's power to respond in the positive ways you desire.

4. *When your mind wanders, bring it back to your point of focus.* This is the step most students forget. They'll complain to me, "I just can't meditate. Every time I try, my mind wanders to other things." I reassure them that they are not unique; they have healthy, normal minds. Everybody's mind wanders. It is the nature of the mind to want to think about other things.

If a two-year-old wasn't getting into mischief, you would worry. The same is true with the mind, and to be a good meditator you need to act like a good parent. As you would firmly but lovingly retrieve the child and bring him back to safety, you must firmly and lovingly, and nonjudgmentally, keep bringing your mind back to your point of focus.

So the challenge is not to keep your mind from wandering, but to *consistently bring it back to your point of focus.* With steady practice, the mind does become more accustomed to remaining still. However, even swamis who meditate on a regular basis, a minimum of three hours a day, have told me they still have to bring the mind back to focus at times.

So don't be put off by the mind's natural tendency to wander. With continued practice, you'll become increasingly able to keep it focused.

OTHER BENEFITS OF MEDITATION

There are many other benefits besides enhancing visualization. You will be increasing your power of concentration, a valuable talent in many parts of life. Meditators tend to have greater ability to learn new tasks, as well as to recall information already learned.

They also report access to another form of information, which they describe as being able to solve problems intuitively. Dr. Deepak Chopra writes in his book, *Creating Health: Beyond Prevention Toward Perfection,* that if he could recommend only one healthy practice to his patients, it would be to meditate every day.

THE MENTAL AND
SPIRITUAL APPROACH

As we begin to use relaxation and meditation in our program, we automatically move into a body/mind/spirit perspective.

Like deep relaxation, effective meditation and visualization cannot be used effectively without a body/mind focus. In *Beyond the Relaxation Response,* however, Dr. Benson discovered the importance of a spiritual element of meditation as well. When he had begun his first studies at Harvard, he didn't want to offend anyone (and I'm sure he didn't want to appear weird himself). So he chose to teach meditation, by suggesting his patients focus on the number "one," a word that he felt would be emotionally neutral to most people, patients and colleagues alike.

However his later works showed that meditation became a deeper and more useful experience when his patients used a theme from their own spiritual life. He called it the "faith factor." And that's the clue. The word or phrase used has to fit each person's belief system. To teach a Christian a Hindu prayer might not work. To teach a Moslem a Jewish prayer might create anything but a peaceful response.

I have found students who particularly liked to use sacred phrases from religions other than their own. But the point is that they make this choice, rather than having it imposed upon them.

SACRED SOUNDS

In fact, this is the way of Sufism. Sufism was traditionally a religion taken from Mohammedan mysticism, but in this country it is practiced through embracing universal teachings from many religions. The Sufis believe, therefore, that sacred sounds from all religions (whether chanted aloud or in silence) create a meditative effect. They believe there is an eternal, divine aspect to every sacred sound, and that this is the quality which opens the heart to receive love and healing.

Interestingly enough just saying the words: "Om," "Amen," "Amin," and "Shalom," all from different religions, have the same physiological effect on the brain and nervous system.

You might try them yourself: Begin the deep three-part breath we covered earlier. On the exhalation sound one of the words. Do this repeatedly, sounding the word you've chosen with each long exhalation. Then do this with each of the other words in turn about five times, or until you feel some effect. Change to another of the words and repeat in the same manner. Notice how you feel.

The yogis have always said that "Om" does not mean peace, it *creates* peace. They are talking about this physiological response.

But you should use whatever term or word brings peace to you. For some people it is a simple humming sound.

MAXIMIZING SPIRITUAL GAINS

There are lots of ways to maximize spiritual gains. One way is by meditating and visualizing in a group. Group experience provides structure and framework, but it does more. When other people meditate with you, you can pick up their energy, and it can take you deeper into the meditative state.

If you can't meditate with people, go to places where people pray, sit in silence and/or meditate. Churches, shrines, synagogues (even mountain tops) often can heighten your experience.

SEND YOUR PRACTICE TO OTHERS

When I first introduced visualization to my heart patients, they were not receptive. "I can't see my heart," one said. "It's a waste of time," said another. "I just don't believe in it," was another response.

Then weeks later during our group meeting, one member of the group told us that he had been diagnosed with prostate cancer. He was very upset. A seven-hour operation was scheduled, and he had been told he could expect significant blood loss. Sharing this with the group, he explained that his greatest fear was not of the operation or the cancer, but of the prospective blood transfusions he would require. The doctors estimated seven or eight units of blood.

At the next class, I suggested that instead of focusing the visualization on our own hearts, perhaps we could send some healing energy to this one member of the group. After getting his permission, we used his suggested imagery—experiencing the blood moving away from his incision, like a river drying in a desert.

To my surprise, all the students who had had difficulty imaging their own healing, could easily and willingly direct it to another member in need. And there was a remarkable outcome. Not only did this person come through the surgery and his recovery period ahead of schedule, he required no blood transfusions at all. They gave him back his own unit of blood as a courtesy.

REINFORCED PRAYER

I have had lots of examples of students who couldn't meditate or visualize until they focused on others first. A private client of mine comes to mind. After unsuccessful attempts with different methods, I finally asked her what she would do if a friend far away was ill and needed her help. She said, "I'd pray." I asked her how she would pray, if her friend had a slipped disc like she had. Then I took the words from her prayer and directed them to her ailing back. Since then she has come to like meditation and visualization, but she calls it "reinforced prayer."

How does prayer work and is it a part of our health program? Dennis Jaffe in his book, *Healing From Within* writes, "The healing power of prayer probably stems in part from [a] ritual of self-acceptance and affirmation. By praying, we acknowledge our inner worthiness and regard ourselves as connected to the wider human community."

Dr. Jaffe suggests that prayer may be a form of deep relaxation as well as a form of positive imagery. Prayer has the ability to stimulate positive expectation. And positive expectation is a powerful source of healing and change.

EXERCISE 9–1
LEARNING MEDITATION AND VISUALIZATION

MEDITATION

Sit in a straight chair. Take care that your spine is erect, your shoulders are back, your head centered. Close your eyes and sit in silence a moment. You might begin the deep three-part breathing practice to help quiet yourself even more.

Now pick a point of focus. This could be your breath, or a word or image that's uplifting to you. When your mind wanders, gently bring it back to your point of focus. Continue sitting in silence for fifteen minutes, or whatever other period of time you chose before you started.

VISUALIZATION

(For best results have some one read this to you or make an audio recording of your own voice.)

Now that your mind is focused, direct it in a healthy way to assist in your own healing. If at any time I choose words or images that are not positive or pleasurable for you, please disregard them and use instead your own words or images.

You may continue sitting or you may choose to lie down on the couch or the floor.

Let your mind take you to a place you've always wanted to go . . . A vacation spot that would be beautiful for you this time of year . . . Tahiti .. . . . Yosemite . . . Australia. It could be somewhere close at hand, or some place very far away. Some place you know well, or some place you have never been. It may be a special place from your childhood. You get to choose your own place of beauty.

Picture it very clearly. See its radiance for you—the exquisite colors of the foliage, the ground cover, the sky and clouds. Listen for any special sounds—any water flowing by, the wind gently blowing, the birds singing just for you. Feel the air—its temperature, the perfect degree of moisture, dryness. Let your body bathe in the atmosphere of your selected paradise. You may even experience certain smells and tastes just from this area. Take the time to bring it all into focus, as clearly as you possibly can. Let the beauty of nature completely nourish and support you.

Now see yourself in this special place. As you walk, notice how you walk with ease and grace. You walk with assurance, full of energy and vitality. You feel as healthy as you've ever been in your life.

What type of activity would you like to do here at your vacation spot? Swim? Hike? Dance? Be with a friend? Take the time to experience yourself doing this activity. Notice that you do it with ease, with comfort, with enjoyment.

Now find a perfect place to lie down—a mound of green grass, a small white sand beach warmed to the right temperature, a pile of brightly colored leaves, or a comfortable lounge chair placed there just for you. As you lie down, know you are completely supported and protected in your special spot.

Here you can create an image that deals with healing some part of your body. Be sure whatever you image is positive, enjoyable, and the words you use are in the present tense.

If you like, send some positive messages to yourself. Here are some suggestions. If they do not fit for you, substitute or add ones specific to your needs.

- My body is strong through stretching and moving.

- My body relaxes with my focused attention.

- I enjoy eating wholesome food.

- I find the time each day to do the things I know are healthy for me.

- Through my efforts I feel my vitality.

- I am able to be of service to myself and others.

Notice how peaceful you are in your special spot. You are perfectly at home here, the place where you have chosen to be—a place you can visit any time you choose. A place that is always waiting, just for you.

Now bring your awareness back to your breathing, and gradually deepen it. As your breath deepens, feel health and vitality moving through your body, starting from your head, going through your torso, your arms, your legs. Your entire body is filled with vitality and fresh energy.

When you are ready, you might want to stretch and yawn. And when you are ready, begin slowly to open your eyes.

RECOMMENDED MEDITATION AND IMAGERY PROGRAM FOR HEALTH

FOR OPTIMAL HEALTH

1. Fifteen minutes of meditation per day.

2. Five minutes of positive imaging per day. (Like Dr. Ornish, I recommend the meditation first, to focus the mind. Then with a focused mind, apply your images.)

TO FEEL BETTER

1. Begin focusing your mind on whatever you are doing (e.g., cutting carrots, washing your hair). When your mind begins to wander to other things, bring it back to the task at hand.

2. Whenever you feel your mind worrying or scaring you, immediately begin to focus on positive, enjoyable images.

PRECAUTIONS

Be careful where you focus your mind. The yogis say you become what you choose to meditate and visualize on.

PERSONAL MEDITATION AND IMAGERY GOALS

I will do the following meditation practice for _____ minutes each day and notice how I feel.

_____

_____

_____

_____

_____

_____

I will do the following visualization for _____ minutes each day and notice how I feel.

_____

_____

_____

_____

_____

_____

PROGRESS REPORT

Date

_____

What Done

_____

_____

_____

_____

Improvements Noticed

_____

_____

_____

_____

_____

_____

_____

Reported to Whom

_____

FURTHER READING

MEDITATION

BENSON, Herbert. *The Relaxation Response.* New York: William Morrow and Co. Inc., 1975.

BENSON, Herbert. *Beyond the Relaxation Response.* New York: Berkley Books, 2nd ed., 1985.

BORYSENKO, Joan. *Minding the Body, Mending the Mind.* New York: Bantam Books, 1988.

CHOPRA, Deepak. *Creating Health: Beyond Prevention Toward Perfection.* Boston: Houghton Mifflin, 1987.

JAFFE, Dennis T. *Healing From Within: Psychological Techniques to Help the Mind Heal the Body.* New York: Simon and Schuster, Inc., rev. ed., 1986.

ORNISH, Dean. Stress, *Diet, and Your Heart.* New York: New American Library, 1983.

ORNISH, Dean. *Dr. Dean Ornish's Program for Reversing Heart Disease.* New York: Ballantine Books, 1992.

VISUALIZATION

ACHTERBERG, Jeanne. *Imagery in Healing: Shamanism and Modern Medicine.* Boston: New Science Library, 1985.

BRESLER, David. "Mind-Controlled Analgesia: The Inner Way to Pain Control." *Imagination and Healing.* A. A. Sheikh (ed.), New York: Baywood Publishing Co., Inc., 1984.

ELIOT, Robert and D. L. Breo. *Is It Worth Dying For?* New York: Bantam Books, 1986.

JAFFE, Dennis T. *Healing From Within: Psychological Techniques to Help the Mind Heal the Body.* New York: Simon and Schuster, Inc., rev. ed., 1986.

ROSSMAN, Martin L. *Healing Yourself: A Step-By-Step Program for Better Health Through Imagery.* New York: Walker and Company, 1987.

SELIGSON, Marcia. "The Physician of the Future: Freddie the Frog." *New West Magazine.* January, 1977.

SQUIRE, Sally. "The Power of Positive Imagery: Visions to Boost Immunity." *American Health.* (July, 1987): 56–61.

THE
MEDICINES
OF THE
HEART:
What Keeps Us Connected
and Feeling Healthful

A merry heart doeth good like a medicine,
but a broken spirit drieth the bones.
THE BIBLE
Proverbs 17:22

. . . the human body is its own best apothecary and
. . . the most successful prescriptions are those filled
by the body itself.
NORMAN COUSINS
ANATOMY OF AN ILLNESS

There is a Spirit which is pure
and which is beyond old age and death . . .
This is Atman, the Spirit in man.
CHANDOGYA UPANISHAD

LESSON TEN
The Body/Mind/Spirit Connection

The room is filled with flowers; artwork is displayed along the walls. Musicians quietly sing in one corner, while students dressed in colorful party attire place objects on a table. Photographs of grandchildren. Pictures of pets. Albums of music. Passages from Scripture. Excerpts from poems. This is our "Celebration of Health," the last class of each *Health and Wholeness* series.

And what we are doing has relevance. Have you noticed how your best friend lifts your spirit? How an evening at the symphony nourishes your soul? How your little short-legged dachshund brings you joy?

These are the medicines of the heart. And in our class we honor their distinctive contributions to our health— completing our journey together toward health and well-being.

WHAT EXACTLY BRINGS US HEALTH AND WELL-BEING?

I'm sure you would agree that there is really more to life and good health than breathing deeply, drinking water, and eating raw carrots. Our task in this final part of our book is to find exactly what that is for each of us, and how we can use it for our health and well-being.

The concept of the "Inner Teacher" is even more important as we explore this chapter, because we'll soon discover that each of us has unique and individual responses to the "medicines of the heart."

197

In fact, what might be one person's magic potion can be another's fatal poison. For instance, when members of my family switch cars, we must be careful to switch music tapes as well. While Zamfir and his pan flute calms and relaxes my nervous system, it has the opposite effect on my childrens'. On the other hand, their favorite selections literally hurt my ears.

FINDING YOUR MAGIC POTION

Take some time right now to notice your preferences and your uniqueness. What calms and nourishes you? To be more precise, exactly what people and what things help you feel vital and filled with a sense of well-being? This could be most anything—talking to your grandchildren, listening to Mozart, wearing "HOT PINK," walking on the beach.

Who or what brings meaning to your life? Your spiritual faith? Volunteering at the day care center? Taking soup to a sick friend?

Who or what helps you feel whole? Helps you raise your spirit? What we're after is exactly what helps you connect better to yourself, to others or to some higher source. For me, I know for sure when its happening, because I want to giggle or cry. Often I get "goose pimples." Emotional energy is moving in me and I can feel it through my body.

When do you get emotionally moved? With whom? Under what conditions?

Now notice how often you make that person, thing, or experience a part of your life. For instance, one trip to the art museum may do more for your soul than ten trips to your doctor. Yet, how often do you find time to sit with

Rembrandt? African flowers are your favorite flower, yet none are in your home. You have this cousin who really makes you laugh, but you see him only at family weddings.

THE IMPORTANCE OF SELF-HEALING

"Medicines of the heart," no matter how simple or bizarre, can be important self-healing influences. Dr. Blair Justice, a psychologist from Rice University, has taught me a great deal about these effects. In his book, *Who Gets Sick: Thinking and Health*, he writes, "[E]vidence suggests that the systems [of our bodies] respond to optimism, caring, intimacy, hope and other positive cognitions." Justice cautions us to notice these effects. "Those who most get sick," he writes, "may be the most out of touch with these self-healing practices."

In the past ten years researchers have been interested in measuring exactly what happens to our bodies while in the presence of these self-healing influences. For the past few years I've tried to organize some of this research into categories for my classes. More important, I've tried to suggest personalized experiments for students to do on their own.

To make it easier to discuss, let's think of this work as falling into seven areas:

1. Giving and Receiving Love

2. Caring for Plants and Pets

3. Being with Family and Friends

4. Enjoying Laughter and Humor

5. Appreciating Music and Beauty

6. Having a Faith

7. Experiencing Hope and Optimism

Let me assure you, however, that these categories are not exclusive. I strongly encourage you to build on them with your own ideas and discoveries.

GIVING AND RECEIVING LOVE

Dr. Bernie Siegel, a surgeon and author of *Love, Medicine and Miracles* has promoted the idea that to improve our health, especially at the time of a life-threatening crisis, we must learn to give our bodies "live" messages. The way to do this, he explains, is to start loving ourselves and others.

"I am convinced," he writes, "that unconditional love is the most powerful known stimulant of the immune system. If I told patients to raise their blood levels of immune globulins or killer T cells, no one would know how. But if I can teach them to love themselves and others fully, the same changes happen automatically."

At the Menninger Clinic in Topeka, Kansas, researchers wanted to find exactly what happens to the body when we love ourselves and others. So they examined the experts— people who were "in love."

Here is what they found. People in love had reduced levels of lactic acid and increased levels of chemicals called endorphins in their blood. This has scientific importance for our well-being. You see, lactic acid in the blood typically makes us feel tired, whereas endorphins make us feel euphoric, and less subject to pain.

These lovers also had fewer colds or other illnesses, because the act of being "in love" had increased the white blood cells that fight off infections.

Receiving Love Enhances the Immune System

We all need love. It is well documented that when babies receive standard physical care in institutions but no special love, their development is slowed, and for some, permanently retarded. Others give up and die. This syndrome is noted clinically as "the failure to thrive."

Dr. Christopher Coe of Stanford found out why. After separating baby monkeys from their mothers, he measured a significant suppression in the infants' immune systems.

The Presence of Love Enhances the Immune System

Actually, it is possible to observe directly the positive effects of love and caring. At Harvard, Drs. David McClelland and Carol Kirshnit asked students to watch different types of movies, while measurements were made of their levels of immunoglobulin-A, a chemical that defends against colds and viruses.

First a Nazi propaganda movie was shown, then a piece on gardening. Neither had any affect on the subjects' immune systems. But a movie showing the violence of Attila the Hun actually lowered their immune reactions.

On the other hand, a movie about Mother Teresa caring for dying people in India produced a sharp increase in the immuno-globulin levels in all the subjects. It was discovered eventually that the students could produce the same effect simply by thinking about people in their lives who had given loving care to them.

Caring Heals

One of my favorite stories is about rabbits who were fed a high-fat diet to see if researchers could induce atherosclerosis (blockage in the coronary arteries). But some of the rabbits got more than just high-fat diets. By accident they discovered that some attendants were talking to and petting certain animals, while just feeding the others. As a result, the report of the study covered more than just diets: The rabbits on the high-fat diet that were talked to and petted developed significantly less atherosclerosis than those which received only the routine laboratory feedings.

But what about touching and caring for people? The *Journal of Personality and Social Psychology* reported faster recoveries for women surgical patients who had their hands held by a nurse while having routine blood pressure and temperatures taken.

Dr. Robert Mack, a surgeon at Swedish Hospital Medical Center in Seattle summarized the underlying principle: "[L]ove cures people, both those who give it and those who receive it."

CARING FOR PETS AND PLANTS

The benefits of caring are not limited to caring for people. They can extend to caring for, or in fact just being in the presence of pets and plants. People with high blood pressure have been able to lower their pressure simply by being in the presence of an animal they love.

Why not try it yourself? Take your blood pressure, play with your pet, then take your blood pressure again. I've noticed that brushing my dog gives me the same internal feeling I get after twenty minutes of meditation.

People who have had heart attacks who own animals have one-half the mortality rate of those who have no pets. Patients in hospitals (including mental hospitals) are reported to recover faster and are discharged sooner when there are pets around. Patients in coronary care units have better survival rates if there are pets waiting for them at home.

At the Center for Attitudinal Healing in Tiburon, California, a place where people with life-threatening illnesses support each other, there is a dog who is acknowledged by the staff as being a co-therapist. Observing this group, I realized what an active participant Fido was. He knew exactly who needed attention and would sit by this person until he received an appropriate emotional response.

While interviewing nurses for my book, *Building Partnerships in Hospital Care*, I was surprised by the number of stories of smuggling pets into intensive care units to assist in the healing of seriously ill patients.

Plants as Healers

Plants have had a healing power as well. Psychologists Ellen Langer, now of Harvard, and Judith Rodin of Yale gave one group of nursing home residents potted plants to care for. Another group was given plants that the staff cared for. Within three weeks, the first group improved in health and increased their over-all activity level. At the end of 18 months, the death rate of the first group was one-half that of the second group.

When I ask students for a list of activities important to their health and well-being, gardening always makes the list. It is no accident that flowers are the messages sent by lovers. Plants can definitely be "medicines of the heart."

BEING WITH FAMILY AND FRIENDS

Have you ever wondered why some people can smoke cigarettes, eat all the wrong foods, never exercise, and yet appear healthy? Well some researchers have had the same questions, and they studied such people to see if there was something they were doing for their health that was not immediately apparent. What they found that each of these people had in common was a strong network of friends.

Personally I believe social support is what makes health promotion work. Would "Weight Watchers" be as effective if its members did not weigh together once a week? Would the Ornish heart patients be able to reduce lesions in their arteries if they weren't part of a supporting group?

Friends are Good Medicine

The California Department of Mental Health developed a program for older adults called "Friends Are Good Medicine." Let me share with you one story where friends actually saved a person's life.

An eighty-year-old woman I call Rosa Browning was not recovering from open heart surgery. Each day she was getting weaker, and her doctor told us she was dying. One day while visiting Rosa, I asked her, "Who makes you feel good to be around?" And I suggested that Rosa visualize these people visiting her in her convalescent hospital room.

As Rosa began listing names, the color in her face noticeably brighten, and sparks of vitality seemed to appear. Just remembering the people who had always given her pleasure appeared to revive the "live" message that Dr. Siegel talked about. A nurse also noted the change. She took me aside and said, "Whatever you're doing, keep it up. Not only can I see it in her face, her vital signs are responding."

Within a few days Rosa and I had devised what we called "Rosa's Get-Well Project." She put together a list of 31 names. Some were close friends, some were long-time acquaintances; but Rosa hadn't limited herself to these. She had listed everyone she felt might help, regardless of how close the relationship. Some were people she barely knew. But in one way or another they'd had some positive influence on her life.

A letter was sent to each of them telling them of their importance to Rosa, and asking them to make a three-month commitment to help Rosa "get well." Each was requested to sign up for one day a month. "On that day," the letter suggested, "you might call Rosa and ask her what she needs. Some days she might need shopping done. Some days she might need someone to talk to. She might ask you to read poetry to her. She might like a home cooked meal. Ask her what she had to eat yesterday, and what type of menu seems appetizing today."

A few days later, these 31 people, mostly strangers to one another, came together for a kickoff party. They met to ask questions, get answers, prepare plans, but mainly to dedicate themselves to an important project.

Within two weeks, Rosa was out of the hospital, and within three months she was recovering. The cardiac surgeon was amazed. He had performed a critical operation; but Rosa, with the help of her friends, had brought herself back to life.

The Care Partner Program

Since then I've seen friends and family have similar influences on patients in hospitals and nursing homes. About seven years ago I approached the Planetree Model Hospital Unit at California Pacific Medical Center to convince them to develop a formal program where loved ones could be recognized members of the hospital health care team. We called the program "The Care Partner Program" (which became the topic of my earlier book).

What interested me from the beginning was not only how the program benefited the patients' health and well-being, but how it helped the care partners and the health workers as well. With family members and friends actually providing personalized caring, institutions can finally accomplish what they're charged to do—provide "health" and "care."

ENJOYING LAUGHTER AND HUMOR

Smile. Did you know you just increased your blood flow to the brain, released the pleasure chemicals in your brain, and reset your autonomic nervous system?

Smiling makes you less reactive to stress. And it's such a simple health technique, one we can easily use several times during the day.

Think of something funny. Now laugh. If you have difficulty, read some jokes. Watch a comedy show. Now, really let go and belly laugh. Can you make your laughter deeper, longer, louder than usual? If you have, you can expect to have stimulated your respiration rate, your heart rate, your muscular activity. You've increased oxygen in your system, and may even have released endorphins and enkephalins, the chemicals in the brain that promote well-being.

Laughter: Internal Jogging

Norman Cousins, the author of *Anatomy of an Illness* and noted authority on positive emotions and health, called laughter "internal jogging." In his effort to heal himself of the collagen disease that he was told would cripple him, he developed a program that included the positive emotions of love, hope, faith, confidence, and laughter.

He found out that ten minutes of laughter a day gave him two hours without pain. It also reduced his sedimentation rates, a laboratory test that served as reinforcement to him that his disease was improving.

Cousins did his research on himself almost thirty years ago; since then, controlled scientific studies have confirmed his conclusions. They have shown that humor and laughter increase antibodies, beta-endorphins, and other pleasure chemicals. They also have an aerobic effect, so important for well-being.

The University of California at Santa Barbara studied laughter. They found it was more effective than biofeedback training in reducing negative physiological effects of stress. As one researcher concluded, ". . . all it requires is a funny bone."

Laughter: Spiritual Healing

Gordon Allport, author of *The Individual and His Religion*, makes another point. "The neurotic who learns to laugh at himself may be on the way to self-management, perhaps cure."

His approach calls to mind the detachment process described in the earlier chapter on progressive deep relaxation. In other words, to be able to laugh at yourself, you must make a cognitive shift that enables you to observe yourself. When you're not so involved in life's vicissitudes, life and your reaction to it actually can look funny. This is why many religious teachers find a spiritual element in self-laughter.

APPRECIATING MUSIC AND BEAUTY

"Would you like a shot of morphine?" the recovery room nurse at the University Hospital in Iowa asks a patient. "No thanks," the patient murmurs. "Just bring me some Tchaikovsky."

Research done at the University of Iowa has demonstrated that patients who listen to music after surgery require less pain medication, are less drowsy, have shorter recoveries, and report a more pleasant hospital experience than those treated with routine narcotics.

Music works at deeper levels than just that of reducing pain. Plato and Aristotle felt it affected the character and soul. The translation of the Greek root word *musike* means art presided over by the gods.

In the Old Testament of the *Bible,* little David played the harp to rid King Saul of evil spirits—apparently an early example of music's use to enhance mental and emotional health. In the eighteenth century, King Philip of Spain called for musicians to lift his recurring depression, enabling him to return to his duties as king.

During our own time studies have shown how music affects, among other things our breathing rate, blood pressure, pulse rate, muscle tension, brain waves, and endorphin production. Music has proved capable of improving learning, sharpening memory, and creating multiple states of consciousness.

Robyn Friedman, a psychotherapist and professional musician, prescribes music to her clients to help them achieve powerful healing states. Some are her selections and some are from Helen Bonny and Louis Savary's book, *Music and Your Mind* are:

Composer or Artist	Title	Feeling/Mood
Copland, Aaron	*Appalachian Spring*	light, buoyant, happy
Denby, Constance	*Sacred Space Music*	nurturing, loving
Grofe, Ferde	*Grand Canyon Suite*	triumphant, serene
Kobialka, Daniel	*Timeless Motion*	peace, joy

Try some experimentation of your own. Sing, play, or listen to music of your choice. When finished, sit in silence a few minutes. See how you feel. How were you affected physically, emotionally, spiritually? Did you notice how your heart beats lower with some music, speeds up with others?

Release of muscle tension is often the quickest response to recognize. You can try this out with some meditation music. In my classes, I often use Steven Halpern's *Spectrum Suite*. Just listen for a few minutes. Notice how relaxed your muscles have become.

209

Then when you're ready, try some Souza marches or Michael Jackson tunes. They can help you to build muscle tension quickly. In fact, certain music makes you feel stronger than you actually are. Just think how march music is used to reinforce military training, how rock music is used to heighten the degree of aerobic exercise.

Once you are aware of your particular body's response to various types of music, you can select what you need— to reduce pain, to lower blood pressure, to increase energy levels, to have that special physiologic effect at important moments.

Beauty for Health

Abraham Maslow, a humanistic psychologist and author, was not so interested in what caused people to be sick, as what allowed them to excel. One aspect of his work emphasized the importance of beauty for health. When we are moved by music, the beauty of nature or a work of art, research has demonstrated that such experiences also release endorphins in our brain.

In a similar way, nature scenes reduce anxiety and increase alpha brain waves. One researcher decided to test this hypothesis in a hospital setting, with patients who were recovering from gall bladder surgery.

Twenty-three of them were given rooms that overlooked beautiful trees with foliage. Twenty-three similar patients were given rooms that looked out on a brick wall. By now I'm sure the results are of no surprise to you. The ones with the nature views required less pain medication, had fewer negative ratings from nurses, and were discharged sooner than those who had looked at the wall.

Some writers believe that color has such healing qualities that people, whether they know it or not, crave to be near certain tones and hues. It's as if we need color to nourish our souls, like we need food to nourish our bodies.

What is beautiful to you? How often are you aware of being in the midst of beauty?

HAVING A FAITH

My anesthesiologist husband loves to give ministers, rabbis, and meditators anesthesia. Why? He started noticing that they required less anesthesia than other people who were undergoing the same operations. With his medical charting he was able to document this recurring situation. How does he explain this? "I believe their faith provided a source of peace which was to them a higher form of medicine."

In the chapter on meditation we talked about Herbert Benson's discovery of the "faith factor." At Harvard Medical School, he teaches prayer (based on the person's belief system) as a way of improving health.

Bernie Siegel tells the story of a patient named Stephanie, who was diagnosed with cancer. Her doctor gave her the grim report with the words, "All you've got is a hope and a prayer." To his surprise she actually followed his advice and was successful in altering the course of her disease. In fact, she improved beyond medical expectations. "[The doctor]," she explained, "was actually prescribing the one medication that was going to cure me, *and he never even knew it.*"

Having a faith, no matter what it is, is equivalent, I believe, to knowing how to ride a surf board. The ocean of life can be very hard without one. The big waves can be overwhelming, knocking you around, pulling you underwater, crashing you against the rocks. But if you can use the surf board of faith, you can ride almost any wave safely into shore.

It's not that your life is any easier. You get the big waves too. The difference is that with your faith to support you you can move forward with the forces of life.

Good Health and Church Attendance

Even church attendance seems to be positively correlated with good health. Church goers have been found in various studies to be less prone to pulmonary emphysema, cirrhosis of the liver, abnormal cervical cytology, and lower blood pressure.

In one study of 800 black parishioners surveyed in Norfolk, Virginia, researchers found less depression among those with active church involvement.

Faith Can Be in Anything

But having faith is not limited to participation in organized religions. Faith can be in anything—in God, in a particular doctor, a special health promotion practice, a certain drug or medical treatment, even in one's own inner strength.

In the chapter on meditation and positive imagery, Dennis Jaffe compared prayer to focusing the mind on a positive outcome. Blair Justice explains faith as a way of having inner control over external factors.

He refers to the way faith can get people through even the harshest of circumstances. "Some people are subjected to harsher circumstances than others are, such as war, racism, poverty, unemployment or age. But . . . even under extreme conditions, it is possible not only to survive but to retain some sense of health and well-being . . . Inner control seem to come easier for those who have a strong faith."

EXPERIENCING HOPE AND OPTIMISM

"Doctors have been telling me for years that you can't kill a happy man," reports Bruce Larsen, a Seattle clergyman. Research consistently proves that people live longer who characteristically have a sense of hope, order, and control in their lives. Louis Gottschalk at the University of California at Irvine found that patients with metastasized cancer who remained hopeful lived longer than others who did not.

Optimism can promote health. Research has shown repeatedly that patients who are optimistic about their own health have reduced death rates—even when laboratory tests and doctors' evaluations indicate they should be at greater risk.

In one dramatic study, 6,928 adults were studied for 9 years in Alameda County, California. For men, the mortality rate for the "health pessimists" was two times greater than for the "health optimists." For women, the mortality rates were five times greater.

Hope and Optimism Can Be Learned

The good news is that we can all learn to be "health optimists." The National Institute of Mental Health in

213

Israel is demonstrating that hope and optimism need not be limited to a few, but can be learned by anyone.

How? One effective way is to practice the health promotion techniques recommended in this book. Most specifically, hope and optimism can be fostered significantly through the use of positive imagery as described in the previous chapter.

DURING DIFFICULT TIMES

A few years ago I had a student who always came to class full of energy and excitement. Margaret always had something inspiring to say. Her smile filled up the room. To me she was an example of "health and wholeness." Three weeks after the class was over, I read in the newspaper that she had died.

What I hadn't known, what very few students had known, was that Margaret had been very ill. She had been in the advanced stages of emphysema, and could only leave her oxygen machine for a couple of hours to come to our class.

Even now I think of her as one of the healthiest people I have ever known. From my point of view she died in health.

She is an eloquent example for me of the fact that the *Health and Wholeness* practices are important to stay healthy to be sure, but they can be perhaps even more important during difficult times.

DIFFICULT TIMES BRUISE

Difficult times can come during illness or following the death of someone we love. But they can also occur after

214

any major disappointment—in fact, during any time of emotional upheaval or stress.

As Tevye said in *Fiddler on the Roof*, life has a way of "confusing us, blessing and bruising us." During the "bruising," in whatever form that comes, I strongly urge the use of the material in this book.

DIFFICULT TIMES LOWER RESISTANCE

One of the questions Bernie Siegel always asks his cancer patients is: What happened to you in the year or two before your illness? There is a scientific reason for his curiosity.

You see, cancer cells are developing in our bodies all of the time. When we are healthy, they are destroyed before they can develop into tumors by the white blood cells that are part of our immune system. Cancer, AIDS, and other diseases often develop when our immune systems are for some reason ineffective. There is strong evidence that emotions of grief, feelings of failure, and suppression of anger can play a role in this immune system failure.

Our job, therefore, is to recognize when we are going through difficult times, so we can be especially good to ourselves. This is not self-indulgence, it is basic good sense. Any stressful event, if experienced over time without any positive intervention, can potentially wear our bodies down and cause premature aging, even death.

WHILE IN HOSPITALS AND NURSING HOMES

Protecting our health is extremely important while undergoing medical treatment. It is well documented that hospitals routinely inflict social, emotional and spiritual pain. Despite the best of intentions, our health care institutions by the very manner in which they operate do things which are actually counterproductive to promoting health. They remove our clothes, take away our possessions, limit our opportunities to be with loved ones, restrict our expressions of personal feelings and our opportunities for learning, laughter, and growth.

Until our hospitals and nursing homes become aware of our social, spiritual and emotional needs, and treat them along with our physical needs, we must take responsibility for providing that kind of healing treatment ourselves. In my book, *Building Partnerships in Hospital Care,* I spell out how individual people like you and me can work with professionals to bring into hospital environments things that keep us whole—art and beauty, laughter and humor, family and friends, faith, hope and optimism.

ACCEPTING LIFE AND STAYING WHOLE

What's important for *Health and Wholeness* is taking responsibility for the things we can do to improve our lives, while accepting what life may bring our way. Since exerting a sense of control is so important in maintaining health, we need a way to still have influence when we are dealing with difficult situations beyond our control.

During major life crises, I strongly suggest surrounding yourself with the things that you've discovered help keep you well. Notice who or what keeps you well: the people you love; your favorite flowers; colors; music; people who make you laugh; things that help your heart to sing. And for your *Health and Wholeness,* place them directly in your life.

216

EXERCISE 10–1
"MEDICINES OF THE HEART"

(For optimal results, make your prescriptions as specific and as enjoyable as possible.)

❦ Some new ways I can give love to others:

_____

❦ Some better ways I can learn to receive love:

_____

❦ Some ways I can care for (or be around) animals and/or pets of my liking:

_____

❦ Some ways I can care for (or be around) my favorite plants:

_____

❦ Names of people who bring joy to me:

_____

❦ Some creative ways to seek these people out:

_____

❦ Some new ways I can experience more laughter and humor:

_____

❦ Some music I need to hear on a regular basis:

_____

❦ Some beauty (artwork or nature) I want to enjoy regularly:

_____

❦ Some colors to surround me each day:

_____

❦ What is my faith and how I can enhance it?

_____

❦ Some ways to practice hope and optimism:

_____

STAYING WELL THROUGH THE BODY/MIND AND SPIRIT

Thus, scientific research has shown how having a sense of control can trigger internal healing mechanisms which lead directly to health and well-being. The five-point program described in this book shows us what to do.

Through eating well, exercising regularly, and practicing the various stress management strategies in this book, we can develop more control over our bodies and how we feel, we can take more control over our mind and how we perceive external threats. By noticing what brings joy to our hearts, we can enhance the spiritual aspects of our lives—giving rise to more love, more faith, more beauty.

And we can stay healthy through the body, mind and spirit—both as we live and when we die.

Health and Wholeness is, you see, more than freedom from disease. It is accepting and enjoying life.

I am wishing you and those you love this kind of life.

FURTHER READING

GIVING AND RECEIVING LOVE

SEIGEL, Bernie S. *Love, Medicine and Miracles: Lessons Learned About Self-Healing From a Surgeon's Experience with Exceptional Patients.* New York: Harper & Row, 1986, pp. 182, 183.

Receiving Love Enhances the Immune System

SEIGEL, 1986, p. 183.

The Presence of Love Enhances the Immune System

McCLELLAND, D.C. *Motivation and Immune Function in Health and Disease.* (March, 1985.) Paper presented at the meeting of the Society of Behavioral Medicine, New Orleans.

Caring Heals

MACK, R. "Occasional Notes: Lessons From Living with Cancer," *New England Journal of Medicine.* (1984):311(25), 1642–1643.

NEREM, R.M., M. J. Levesque, and J. F. Cornhill. "Social Environment as a Factor in Diet-Induced Atherosclerosis." *Science.* (1980): 208(4452), 1475–1476.

WHITCHER, S. J., and J. D. Fisher. "Multidimensional Reaction to Therapeutic Touch in a Hospital Setting." *Journal of Personality and Social Psychology.* (1979): 37(1), 87–96.

CARING FOR PETS

ANGIER, N. "Four-Legged Therapists." *Discover.* (August, 1983): 86–89.

220

MESSENI, P. *Panel on Pets as Social Support.* (June, 1984.) Meeting of the Pacific division of the American Association for the Advancement of Science, San Francisco.

MINKLER, M. *Social Networks and Health: People Need People, 1983.* (Series on the Healing Brain Cassette Recording No. T57). Los Altos, CA: Institute for Study of Human Knowledge.

CARING FOR PLANTS

LANGER, E.J. and J. Rodin. "The Effects of Choice and Enhanced Personal Responsibility For the Aged: A Field Experiment in a Institutional Setting." *Journal of Personality and Social Psychology.* (1976): 34, 191–198.

BEING WITH FAMILY AND FRIENDS

MINKLER, M. *Social Networks and Health: People Need People, 1983.* (Series on the Healing Brain Cassette Recording No. T57). Los Altos, CA: Institute for Study of Human Knowledge.

The Care Partner Program

SCHELLER, Mary Dale. *Building Partnerships in Hospital Care: Empowering Patients, Families and Professionals.* Palo Alto, CA: Bull Publishing Co., 1990, pp. 11–13; 147–152.

ENJOYING LAUGHTER AND HUMOR

FRY, W. F. Jr., and P. E. Stoft. "Mirth and Oxygen Saturation Levels of Peripheral Blood." *Psychotherapy and Psychosomatics.* (1971): 19, 76–84.

Laughter: Internal Jogging

COUSINS, Norman. *Anatomy of an Illness: As Perceived by the Patient, Reflections on Healing and Regeneration.* New York: Bantam Books, 1981.

DILLON, K.M., B. Minchoff, and K. H. Baker. "Positive Emotional States and Enhancement of the Immune System," *International Journal of Psychiatry in Medicine.* (1985–86) 15(1), 13–18.

FRY, W.F. Jr. and P.E. Stoft. "Mirth and Oxygen Saturation Levels of Peripheral Blood." *Psychotherapy and Psychosomatics.* (1971): 19, 76–84.

LEVI, L. "The Urinary Output of Adrenalin and Noradrenalin During Pleasant and Unpleasant Emotional States," *Psychosomatic Medicine.* (1965): 27: 80–85.

Laughter: Spiritual Healing

ALLPORT, Gordon W. *The Individual and His Religion.* New York: The Macmillan Co., 1956, p. 92.

APPRECIATING MUSIC

BONNY, Helen and Louis Savary. *Music and Your Mind,* New York: Harper & Row, 1973.

FRIEDMAN, Robyn. "Music and Healing," *Health Lecture Series.* The Planetree Health Resource Center, San Francisco, (October 12, 1989.)

GOLDSTEIN, A. "Thrills in Response to Music and Other Stimuli." *Physiological Psychology,* (1980): 8(1): 126–129.

"Kill Pain With Shot of Music," *Marin Independent Journal* (March 30, 1989).

SEIGEL, 1986, pp. 50, 51.

Beauty for Health

DUDA, Deborah. *A Guide to Dying At Home.* Santa Fe: John Muir Publications, 1982.

GOLDSTEIN, A., 1980, pp. 126–129.

MASLOW, Abraham. *The Farther Reaches of Human Nature.* New York: Viking, 1971.

ULRICH, R.S. "Natural Versus Urban Scenes: Some Psychophysiological Effects." *Environment and Behavior.* (1981): 13(5), 523–556.

ULRICH, R.S. "View Through a Window May Influence Recovery From Surgery." *Science.* (1984): 224(4647), 420–421.

ULRICH, R.S. "Visual Landscapes and Psychological Well-Being," *Landscape Research.* (1979): 4, 17–23.

HAVING A FAITH

BENSON, Herbert. *Beyond the Relaxation Response.* New York: Berkley Books, 2nd ed., 1985, pp. 103–117.

SEIGEL, 1986, p, 38.

Good Health and Church Attendance

COMSTOCK, G. W., and K. B. Partridge. "Church Attendance and Health." *Journal of Chronic Diseases.* (1972): 25: 665–672.

GRAHAM, T.W., B. H. Kaplan, J. C. Cornoni-Huntley, S.A. James, C. Becker, C. G. Hames, and S. Hayden. "Frequency of Church Attendance and Blood Pressure Elevation." *Journal of Behavioral Medicine.* (1978): 1(1): 37–43.

WATTS, R. J., N. G. Milburn, D. R. Brown, and L. E. Gary. *Epidemiological Research on Blacks and Depression: A Sociocultural Perspec-tive.* (November, 1985.) Paper presented at the annual meeting of the American Public Health Association, Washington, D.C.

Faith Can Be in Anything

JUSTICE, Blair. *Who Gets Sick: Thinking and Health.* Houston: Peak Press, 1987, pp. 128–140, 256–272.

EXPERIENCING HOPE AND OPTIMISM

EASTMAN, P. "How to Live a Long Life: Psychological vs. Physiological Aspects of Growing Old." *Houston Post.* (July 23, 1985): 5B, 8B.

GOTTSCHALK, L.A. "Hope and Other Deterrents to Illness." *American Journal of Psychotherapy.* (1985): 39(4): 515–524.

KAPLAN, G.A., and T. Camacho. "Perceived Health and Mortality: A Nine-Year Follow-Up of the Human Population Laboratory Cohort," *American Journal of Epidemiology.* (1983): 117(3): 292–304.

LARSON, Bruce. *There's a Lot More to Health Than Not Being Sick.* Waco, Texas: Word Books, (1984) p. 123.

MOSSEY, J. A., and E. Shapiro. "Self-Rated Health: A Predictor of Mortality Among the Elderly." *American Journal of Public Health.* (1982): 72(8), 800–808.

VAILLANT, G.E. "Natural History of Male Psychologic Health: Effects of Mental Health on Physical Health," *New England Journal of Medicine.* (1979): 301(23), 1249–1254.

Hope and Optimism Can Be Learned

EASTMAN, P., 1985, pp. 5B, 8B.

DURING DIFFICULT TIMES:
WHILE IN HOSPITALS AND NURSING HOMES

KALISH, Richard. "The Effects of Death Upon the Family." *Death and Dying.* Leonard Pearson (ed.). Cleveland, Ohio: Case Western Reserve University, 1969.

SCHELLER, 1990, pp. 227, 228.

WOODSON, Robert. "Hospice Care in Terminal Illness." *Psychosocial Care of the Dying Patient.* Charles A. Garfield (ed.). New York: McGraw Hill Book Co., 1978.

COPYRIGHT ACKNOWLEDGEMENTS

Grateful acknowledgement is made to the following for permission to quote from copyrighted material:

INTRODUCTION

Travis, John and Regina Sara Ryan. *Illness/Wellness Continuum.* Used with permission from Wellness Associates, Ukiah, CA.

POINT ONE
Deep Breathing: *How Did We Live Without It?*

Excerpt from *Prayers of the Cosomos* by Neil Douglas-Klotz. Copyright 1990 by Neil Douglas-Klotz. Reprinted by permission of HarperCollins Publishers.

POINT THREE
Dining with the *"Inner Teacher": A New Approach to Eating Well and Drinking Water*

Austin, Mary. *The Textbook of Acupuncture Therapy.* 1972.

Pelletier, Kenneth. *Longevity: Fulfilling Our Biological Potential.* Dell Publishing Company. 1981. Used with permission.

Fries, James F. and Lawrence M. Crapo. *Vitality and Aging.* W. H. Freeman and Company. 1981. Used with permission.

Guthrie, Helen. *Introductory Nutrition.* C. V. Mosby Co., St. Louis, MO. 1971. Used with permission.

Finlay, Steven. "How to Bridge Your Water Gulf: Like Troops You May Need a Drink," *U.S. News & World Report*, October 22, 1990. Used with permission.

POINT FOUR
The Art of Relaxation

The material on pages 135-137 is taken in substance from *The Integral Yoga Teacher's Training Manual,* copyright 1983 and subsequently by Satchidananda Ashram—Yogaville. Used with permission.

Chang, Stephan. *The Complete Book of Acupuncture.* Reprinted by permission of Celestial Arts, Berkeley, CA.

POINT FIVE
Maintaining a Focused Mind and a Positive Attitude

Bresler, David. "Mind Controlled Analgesia: The Inner Way to Pain Control" from *Imagination and Healing.* Baywood Publishing Co., Inc. 1984. Used with permission.

Jaffe, Dennis. *Healing from Within.* Random House, Inc. 1986. Used with permission.

PART THREE
THE MEDICINES OF THE HEART:
What Keeps Us Connected and Feeling Healthful

Cousins, Norman. *The Anatomy of an Illness.* W. W. Norton & Company, Inc. 1981. Used with permission.

Justice, Blair. *Who Gets Sick: Thinking and Healing.* Peak Press. 1987. Used with permission.

Siegel, Bernie. *Love, Medicine & Miracles.* HarperCollins Publishers. 1986. Used with permission.

Excerpted from information in *NEJM,* "Occasional Notes: Lessons from Living with Cancer," by Robert Mack. Issue 311 (25) 1642-1643, 1984. Used with permission.

"Laughing Toward Longevity," excerpted from University of California, Berkeley *Wellness Letter* Health Associated, 1992. Used with permission.

Allport, Gordon. *The Individual and His Religion.* Macmillan Publishing Co. 1956. Used with permission.

ACKNOWLEDGEMENTS

Friedman, Robyn. Musical Selections. From a seminar handout. Used with permission.

Bonny, Helen and Louis Savary. *Music and Your Mind*. HarperCollins Publishers. 1973. Used with permission.

Index

A

B

C

F

I

N

R

S

U

V

W

Y

Z

Building Partnerships in Hospital Care

Empowering Patients, Families
& Professionals

MARY DALE SCHELLER, M.S.W.

*A milestone in revolutionizing health care . . . Every patient
going into a hospital should read this book. Every nurse and
doctor working inside an institution* must *read this book.*

ECHO HERON, R.N.
Best-selling author of
Intensive Care: The Story of a Nurse

———————— ❧ ————————

IN *Building Partnerships in Hospital Care,* Mary Dales
lays out a step-by-step plan for raising the quality of
human caring for everyone who must spend time in
hospitals and nursing homes—patients and visitors
as well as health care professionals. Her unique "care partner program" draws the patient, a relative or friend, and a
professional of the patient's own choosing into a mutually
caring, healing partnership, to care for patients' emotional
and psychological needs as well as their medical needs.

Scheller's goal is simple. She aims to *desensitize* patients
and families to their fears of illness, hospital machinery,
and authority figures. At the same time, she seeks to *resen-
sitize* institution-weary professionals to the feelings, instincts, and emotions that brought them into the field in
the first place. The object is to help all members of the partnership to change negative attitudes and behavior, and by

so doing, change how they experience the institution and each other.

Scheller developed the care partner concept while caring for her own father in a hospital and nursing home. She subsequently designed a formal program for the internationally-recognized Planetree Model Hospital Unit at California Pacific Medical Center in San Francisco.

ORDER FORM

Bull Publishing Company
P.O. Box 208
Palo Alto, CA 94302-0208

(415) 322-2855
Toll Free 1-800-676-2855
Fax (415) 327-3300

Please send me:

_____ *Building Partnerships in Hospital Care* @ $10.95 _____

_____ *Growing Older/Feeling Better* @ $12.95 _____

Subtotal _____

CA residents add 8.5% sales tax _____

Shipping: $3.00 first book;
$.75 each additional _____

TOTAL _____

All orders must be prepaid.

_____ My check is enclosed

_____ Please charge my Visa or MasterCard

Card # _____ Exp. _____

Signature _____

Name _____

Address _____

City _____ State _____ Zip _____

Phone _____

ORDER FORM

Bull Publishing Company
P.O. Box 208
Palo Alto, CA 94302-0208

(415) 322-2855
Toll Free 1-800-676-2855
Fax (415) 327-3300

Please send me:

_____ *Building Partnerships in Hospital Care* @ $10.95 _____

_____ *Growing Older/Feeling Better* @ $12.95 _____

Subtotal _____

CA residents add 8.5% sales tax _____

Shipping: $3.00 first book;
$.75 each additional _____

TOTAL _____

All orders must be prepaid.

_____ My check is enclosed

_____ Please charge my Visa or MasterCard

Card # _____ Exp. _____

Signature _____

Name _____

Address _____

City _____ State _____ Zip _____

Phone _____